FORTUNE-T
BY CRYSTA~~~ ~~~
SEMIPRECIOUS
STONES

A practical guide to the meanings and powers of crystals and stones, and to their use in meditation, healing and the ancient art of divination.

FORTUNE-TELLING BY CRYSTALS AND SEMIPRECIOUS STONES

A Practical Guide to Their Use in Divination, Meditation and Healing

URSULA MARKHAM

THE AQUARIAN PRESS
Wellingborough, Northamptonshire

First published 1987

British Library Cataloguing in Publication Data

Markham, Ursula
Fortune-telling from crystals and semiprecious stones
1. Fortune-telling by precious stones
I. Title
133.3'3   BF1891.P7

ISBN 0-85030-510-1

The Aquarian Press is part of the Thorsons Publishing Group

Printed and bound in Great Britain

Dedication

This book is dedicated with
love to my mother and father

U.M.

'These gems have life in them: their
colours speak,
Say what words fail of.'

George Eliot

Contents

Introduction

'Fortune-telling from ancient stones! Is this some new method just invented?' Such was the typical reaction when first I changed my 'tools' of divination from a pack of tarot cards to a tray of some hundred and fifty beautiful crystals and semiprecious stones.

Far from being a new way of fortune-telling, using crystals and stones is perhaps one of the oldest methods of all. It was known to the Egyptians, the Aztecs and the Incas. In fact, it was reading about those ancient civilizations and their divinatory methods which first started me on the path I now follow.

Just a few short years ago I was given a present. In an ordinary brown cardboard box, placed before me with little ceremony, I found one hundred and fifty glowingly beautiful crystals and stones – ranging in colour from the rich earthy reds of the jasper to the delicate ethereal beauty of the amethyst. The stones had been lovingly polished, but this served only to enhance the natural beauty of their colours and shapes.

These stones were given to me simply as things to be looked at and admired. But, as I began to turn them over in my hand and to wonder at the variety of their shapes and colours, I could not help being aware that they had an energy and a power all of their own and that there was, in fact, a different energy being given off by different individual stones. Some seemed to be quiet and placid, while others were so vibrant and full of life that I felt they might almost burn my fingers.

At the same time, even as I examined my gifts, into my mind flashed snippets from a book I had just finished reading – a book about the ancient civilizations of the Aztecs and the Incas. One small section of the book kept coming into my head – the section which dealt with the way in which those people had used stones for divination – to answer questions, tell of the future and advise their questioners. Coincidence? Years of work in the psychic, spiritual and mystical areas of life had long since persuaded me that coincidence does not exist. I believe that those things which happen are meant to happen. Ideas and thoughts which enter our heads do not come there by chance. Whether or not we ever make use of those ideas and thoughts is another matter – that does not alter the fact that they are given to us for a purpose.

Why shouldn't the stones be given their chance to speak once again? Why shouldn't I begin to use them as they had once been used – to aid divination and to help those who come to see me with questions about their future? The more I thought about it, the more it seemed that this was what I wanted to do.

Perhaps one of the things which most appealed to me about using my lovely crystals and stones was that they were things of nature. True, they had been polished, but this served only to enhance their natural beauty. In view of this, it seemed appropriate to use the tools nature had provided rather than to use cards designed and made by man.

But how to go about it? Even as I looked, some of the stones seemed to shout their meaning to me. The amethyst had such a spiritual air about it; the tiger's eye seemed so strongly independent; the red jasper looked so earthy and emotional. The following days were spent in contemplation and meditation as I 'asked' to be given a meaning for each of the stones. Some of those meanings – such as the ones I have already mentioned – seemed so obvious that I scarcely had to think about them; others took longer to become apparent. But eventually I had a meaning for each and every crystal and stone I possessed. Those meanings had been given to me in the quiet of my own room. It wasn't until much later that I discovered how they were linked to the astrological meanings attributed to crystals and stones. And when I did, it only served to increase my sense of purpose.

The stones were the particular vehicle decreed by fate by which I could best help the people who came to see me. And, even though your stones will not be identical to mine – treasures of nature can never be precisely reproduced – reading this book should enable you to use them as a means of divination to help yourself and others too, as did those ancient seers of civilizations long since past.

You will see in the following pages two lists of crystals and semiprecious stones. The first, on page 15, introduces you to those which have been renowned through the ages for their healing properties, as described in the accompanying text. On page 26 I list the stones which I personally have found most appropriate for divination; their meanings, too, are outlined.

Section I

Crystals and Stones: their Traditional Uses

1. Meditation

Crystals of varying types, as well as certain varieties of stones, can be used to help your ability to meditate and to reach a higher spiritual level. For this purpose, it is essential that you choose a crystal and make it your own. Your meditation crystal should not be widely handled by others, nor should it be left around to collect dust. A crystal of your own is a special friend. It can help you throughout your life and, just like any other good friend, it should be cherished.

Precious and semiprecious stones in general, and crystals in particular, work with man to release cosmic energies to enable him to heal both himself and others and to reach a deeper state of meditation and spiritual understanding. As Win Kent and Jesse H. Thompson say in *Portals of Power* (published by the International Association of Colour Healers):

> To choose a stone, or even be chosen by a stone, relate to its level of consciousness, to focalise the will upon the stone, is to release its cosmic powers, is to tune in and touch the heart of its angelic being.
>
> The gemstone shares its beauty with man and offers the powers of its soul if man will but accept and learn how to use that force.

There are many different ways of choosing your crystal – in fact, quite often, the crystal will seem to choose you. You need a selection of crystals from which to choose. Take your time. This will be an important choice because your crystal can supply the actual and spiritual energy needed to help you in your own personal development.

For those of you who are of a strongly psychic or intuitive

nature, you may find that one particular crystal will seem to 'leap out' at you – will almost ask to be selected. Pick it up. Hold it in the palm of your hand. Close your eyes. What do you feel? Try to relax your mind and your body and open yourself up to the sensations you are experiencing. If that particular crystal is truly meant to belong to you, you should feel either a tingling sensation emitting from the stone or a strong pulsating vibration in the palm of your hand. It may be that you will be fortunate enough to find your own crystal almost immediately but you may have to handle, caress and listen to several before the most appropriate one makes itself felt.

The crystals which are likely to be of the most help to you in meditation and in increasing your spiritual awareness are quartz crystals, amethysts or rose quartz. These were all used in ancient times by seers and soothsayers and men of mystic faith and have long been held to contain their own special properties.

Once you have selected your own crystal you must cleanse and purify it and then charge it to make it your own. Wash the crystal in clear running water and allow it to dry as naturally as possible – preferably in sunlight. In this way the crystal will add to its already considerable energy level the positive energies coming from the rays of the sun.

To charge your crystal and make it truly your own requires peace and solitude. Holding the crystal in the palm of your hand, sit in a comfortable position. Close your eyes, breathe slowly and evenly and relax your body as best you can. Spend a few moments sitting in that relaxed position concentrating on nothing other than the even regularity of your breathing. Very slowly, visualize a circle of white light forming around your feet in a clockwise direction and let this circle of white light build up and up, around your body and your head, layer upon layer, coil upon coil, always in a clockwise direction, until it seals itself in the space immediately above your head. Hold that picture and that position for several minutes, your crystal still in the palm of your hand.

From that time onwards the crystal you have chosen will be yours and yours alone. Keep it with you. Some people like to wear them close to the body, some prefer to carry them on their person in some other way. If you decide to do the latter, it is as well to wrap the crystal in a smooth cloth or to put it into a small pouch in order that it may remain clean and unharmed.

2. Healing

Crystals have been used in healing from the earliest recorded times. Certainly they were used by the Aztec and Inca civilizations and they are also reputed to have been used in the lost continent of Atlantis. The quartz crystal, used as a pendulum, can assist in finding those areas where healing is most needed and it can also be a valuable tool in the pinpointing of vitamin deficiency.

A quartz crystal, pushed into the earth of an ailing potted plant, will often not only revive the plant but take it onward and upward to a strength and vigour hitherto unexpected and unseen. I do not pretend to be able to explain just why this should be, any more than I really understand why music seems to help plants to grow, but I accept one as much as I do the other, having proved both to my own satisfaction in my own home.

For those concerned with healing themselves or others, the following is a list of stones and crystals and the healing properties they are said to possess. In no case is it suggested that crystal healing should replace medical treatment, but it can certainly supplement it and it has been found by many to be beneficial. As I do not have personal knowledge of each and every one of the stones and crystals listed, I am grateful in this section for the help given to me by Phyllis and David Lovell of Crystal World, by Manan and Santoshi of the Fellowship of the Rose and by Falcon Robinson.

3. Crystals and Stones: their Healing Properties

Although none of the crystals and stones listed in the section on how to conduct a psychic reading (page 26) is particularly expensive (indeed prices range from about 50p upwards), you will find that some of those mentioned in the following list are somewhat higher in price. By reading through the list, however, and making your own comparisons, you will find that in many cases there is a choice between stones of lesser and higher cost for counteracting the same ailment. For example, in place of an emerald for overcoming depression, it is quite possible to use a far less expensive bloodstone. To staunch a flow of blood or prevent excessive bleeding one could indeed wear a beautiful blue sapphire, but similar properties are attributed to the humbler carnelian.

For anyone who suffers regularly from a particular ailment,

however, what better choice of engagement ring or special gift could there be than an item of jewellery containing the wearer's own protective stone?

Agate: The agate is said to be a general energy booster, to help increase vitality and confidence in oneself. It is also believed to be of special value for athletes and others who have to call upon sudden bursts of energy, whether physical or mental.

Amber: Amber is not actually a stone but is the fossilized resin of trees. It is reputed to have a particularly beneficial effect when used by those who suffer from infections of the throat, bronchial disorders, asthma or convulsions.

Amethyst: The spiritual stone. The amethyst has long had the reputation of increasing the ability to develop and to evolve spiritually. To sleep with a piece of amethyst beneath one's pillow is said to promote intuitive dreams and inspired thinking. It is also used by many to relieve insomnia and to bring calm in times of grief.

Aquamarine: The aquamarine is used by healers to help overcome problems to do with the eyes, the liver, the throat and the stomach. It is also supposed to promote clear and logical thought and should be carried by those who are taking examinations or being interviewed for employment.

Aventurine: This is said to be useful in relieving migraine and in soothing the eyes. A recommended remedy is to leave a piece of aventurine in water overnight and to use that water the following day to bathe the eyes. Aventurine water, made in the same way, can also be used for bathing skin irritations with a reputedly beneficial effect.

Azurite: It is claimed that the azurite was a stone used as a general healing stone in Atlantis. It is also recommended in the writings of Edgar Cayce as an aid to psychic development.

Beryl: The beryl has been used by healers for centuries to ease complaints of the throat and of the liver.

Bloodstone: The bloodstone is believed to overcome depression and melancholia in the wearer. It is also said to help those who suffer from aches and pains which have an emotional rather than a physical cause.

Carnelian: The carnelian has the reputation of being able to staunch the flow of blood. It can be used when a person is suffering from an open wound. It can be worn in a pouch around the neck by women during menstrual periods and it is said to ease the stomach cramps often brought about by that condition. It is also as good as, if not better than, the traditional remedy of a key placed against the back of the neck of someone who is suffering from a nosebleed.

Chrysocolla: Although the chrysocolla is the stone said to have been used for healing by priests in ancient times, the actual way in which it was used was always kept a closely guarded secret.

Chrysoprase: The chrysoprase is a stone said to improve the memory and to increase presence of mind. It also has the reputation of being able to reduce nervousness and impatience in those who would normally suffer in this way.

Citrine: The citrine is believed to have properties which help to control the emotions and to give a new sense of purpose to those who may feel that they have lost their way in life. It is said to be of help in improving the circulation.

Coral: Coral is said to promote general physical and mental health and to be of particular assistance to those suffering from anaemia. It is also a traditional belief that coral can be used to ward off evil thoughts sent out by ill-wishers and it is still used in this way in many parts of the world.

Emerald: The emerald is reputedly beneficial in overcoming depression and in helping those who suffer from insomnia. It is also said to improve both the memory and the intellect.

Garnet: It is claimed that the garnet is one of the best general tonics for the whole system – mental, physical and emotional. It is particularly recommended to strengthen courage and to increase self-respect and self-confidence.

Jade: Jade is believed to be of the greatest help in relieving uncomfortable kidney complaints. Yellow jade, in particular, is believed to aid a poor digestion. Jade is also thought to provide protection from enemies when worn as a piece of jewellery. It was widely used in Ancient China and Ancient Egypt as a talisman for good fortune and to attract friendship and loyalty.

Jasper: Green jasper has the reputation of being able to improve the sense of smell and to overcome depression, bringing quietness to a troubled mind. Red jasper contains iron oxide (used medically to control excessive bleeding) and therefore, it is claimed, can help in overcoming disorders of the blood and can assist those with a tendency to haemorrhage.

Jet: Jet is not really a stone but is a fossilized plant. It is said to help control and ease migraine and pain behind the eyes.

Lapis lazuli: Called by the Ancient Egyptians 'the Stone of Heavens', the lapis lazuli is thought by many to be the stone upon which were carved the laws given to Moses. It is said to possess the power to prevent fits and epilepsy and also believed to improve the eyesight.

Loadstone: The loadstone is also known as the 'Hercules Stone'. It is widely thought that it can help to heal such ailments as rheumatism, gout, neuralgia, cramp and poor circulation in the legs and feet.

Malachite: It is claimed that the malachite can aid those suffering from asthma, irregular menstruation and depression. It is also believed to contribute to a general feeling of well-being.

Moonstone: The moonstone is said to promote long life and happiness and also to attract loyalty and friendship towards the wearer. It is also often used to reduce excess fluid in the body and to reduce swelling.

Obsidian: The obsidian is actually volcanic lava and is thought to be good for improving the vision. Mystics also believe that it is good for improving the higher vision – that of spiritual awareness.

Onyx: The onyx is believed to improve concentration and devotion and, for this reason, it is to be found on rosaries.

Opal: The opal used to have the reputation of being an unlucky stone but this could be, at least in part, because it induces daydreaming which can, of course, have beneficial or detrimental effects. The daydreamer may lose all sense of reality or he may make use of the 'dream-time' to formulate plans and ideas which will have rewarding results.

Pearl: The pearl is still traditionally worn by divers to protect them from evils of the water, particularly sharks. It is also said to be good for clearing all forms of catarrh, bronchitis, and chest and lung infections.

Peridot: The peridot is said to aid the digestion and to be useful in reducing fever. It is also recommended as a cure for insomnia.

Pyrites: Said to strengthen the circulatory system and to increase the oxygen supply in the blood, pyrites is also believed to be useful in clearing congested air passages.

Quartz (rock crystal): The greatest attribute of the quartz crystal is known to be its use as an aid to opening the psychic centres, to enabling one to meditate at a deeper level and to freeing the mind from the mundane. It releases the individual's higher consciousness and assists in the development of all kinds of mystical and spiritual gifts. The rock crystal attracts the powers of light and energy and is an excellent general healer.

Rose quartz: This beautiful pink stone is said to stimulate the imagination and the intellect. The rose quartz is also reputed to be one of the best stones to use in curing migraine and other headaches.

Ruby: The ruby is thought to increase energy levels and is often used to alleviate disorders of the blood – anaemia, poor circulation, etc. It is also thought to be an aid to intuitive thinking.

Rutilated quartz: Often used in conjunction with beryl, the rutilated quartz is said to be of particular benefit to those who suffer from chestiness in the form of bronchitis, asthma, etc.

Sapphire: Many healing qualities are attributed to the sapphire. In the physical sense it is used in helping to overcome such problems as backache and skin disorders, to improve the condition of the hair and the nails, and to prevent bleeding. There have also been claims that it can assist in the treatment of certain types of cancer. On an emotional level, the sapphire is said to promote an intensity of loving feeling, to give the wearer the qualities of devotion, self-esteem, purity of mind and contentment.

Serpentina: The serpentina is believed to increase both the wisdom and the self-restraint of the bearer. This stone should always be worn attached to a cord rather than a chain.

Smokey quartz: The smokey quartz has been used for centuries as a good-luck charm or talisman and its qualities are thought to lie more in this direction than in that of healing.

Sodalite: The blue sodalite is thought to assist in the lowering of blood-pressure and to have a cooling effect upon those suffering from a high temperature or a fever.

Spinel: The spinel is said to increase the inner strength and character of the one who wears it and also to attract to that person help when help is needed.

Staurolite (The Fairy Stone): Generally reputed to be beneficial for those feeling 'under the weather' with no apparent cause, the fairy stone is also valued by many as a token of good fortune, probably because of the markings of the cross which can be seen on it.

Tiger's eye: The tiger's eye is said to be powerful against hypochondria and psychosomatic diseases and to impart a feeling of confidence and inner strength to the wearer, helping him to know and understand himself more thoroughly. There are some who also believe it to be of help in healing conditions of the eye, but there is not a great deal of support for this claim and it may well be that the connection is really because of the name of the stone.

Topaz: The topaz is said to help to relieve high blood pressure and to reduce varicose veins. It is also thought to encourage sound, dreamless sleep and to prevent insomnia. There are those who consider the topaz to prevent baldness, but very little substantiation has been found for this claim.

Tourmaline: The tourmaline, or 'confidence stone' is strongly believed to relieve nervousness in the wearer and to encourage self-assurance. The tourmaline should be worn against the skin for maximum effect.

Turquoise: The turquoise is still considered by some American Indians to be sacred. It is thought to absorb harmful vibrations and is therefore used as a stone of protection. A turquoise should always be given by another and not purchased for oneself. It was at one time frequently given to those about to undergo surgery as a form of protection during the operation.

Zircon: The zircon is believed to be helpful in increasing the appetite and in overcoming complaints of the liver.

4. How to Use your Stones or Crystals in Self-Healing

Lie on a bed or sit in a comfortable chair in a quiet place where you are not likely to be disturbed. Consciously relax your body, starting from your feet and working upwards towards your head. Let your breathing become easy and regular and focus your complete attention upon the stone or crystal you have chosen, which should be lying in the palm of your hand. Really concentrate on the stone, its shape, its colour, its texture. Then close your eyes – you should still be able to see the stone quite clearly in your mind. Now it is time to visualize the coloured rays from the stone being directed towards the area of your body which you feel is in need of healing. If you have been concentrating sufficiently, you should feel a warm glow around the distressed area itself.

Remember that stones and crystals used in this way for healing should always be used in addition to any treatment – whether traditional or complementary – that has been prescribed for you, and never as a substitute. Their task is to speed the healing process and augment the effects of any treatment you may be undergoing.

5. Crystals, Stones and Astrology

It has long been accepted that each sign of the zodiac has its own particular stone or crystal relating to it. It should follow, therefore, that those born under a particular sign should gain most benefit from wearing the appropriate stone. However, just as the astrological chart takes into account the position of all the planets at the time of birth, so each individual is made up of characteristics taken from the different signs of the zodiac. It is not, therefore, advisable to choose your personal stone merely because of the date on a calendar on the day you were born, but by studying the characteristics of each particular sign, noting which description seems to apply most aptly to you and choosing the stone allied to that particular description. It may even be that, as time progresses and your nature and temperament alter, you will feel happier wearing a variety of different stones at different stages of your life.

Given below are the characteristics generally attributed to each particular sign of the zodiac and the stone or stones normally considered most beneficial for people with those characteristics. I am grateful here for the help of Jill Bruce and also for information learned from Derek and Julia Parker's book *The Compleat Astrologer*.

Aries: Those with a strong Arian influence are direct, lively-minded people, generous and freedom-loving. They can also be quick-tempered (but seldom bear grudges) and impatient and may appear to others to be less than subtle in their approach to matters. If you are an Aries-type, the most appropriate stone would be the diamond, the ruby or – less expensively perhaps – the red jasper.

Taurus: The Taurean type is solid, determined and practical. He will have a love of luxury – perhaps to the point of self-indulgence at times – and can be somewhat fanatical about routine. Nevertheless, he is both warm-hearted and trustworthy and will probably have an excellent sense of business. If you are the Taurus-type, your most appropriate stone would be either the sapphire or the lapis lazuli.

Gemini: The Geminian is the complete communicator. Whether it be in a small way, by speaking, writing letters or even indulging in gossip, or whether he becomes a journalist, a lecturer, a broadcaster or an author, the Gemini-type *has* to spread his thoughts and ideas far and wide. As a person, he will probably be lively, versatile and amusing, although he can also show indications of the other side of this coin and become restless, living on nervous energy and changeable in his emotions. If this is your nature, the stone that you should choose should be either the citrine or one of the yellow agates.

Cancer: Just like the crab, the Cancer-type is hard shell on the outside and soft and vulnerable on the inside. To others he may appear to be over-sensitive, moody and touchy but inside he is suffering for those he cares about more than for himself. He is kind and sympathetic and very protective of his own family. He is also an excellent home-maker and will love and cherish his home and those who inhabit it. If you are Cancerian in type, your ideal stone would be either a pearl or a moonstone.

Leo: The Leonine nature is the 'centre-stage' nature. The Leo-type loves to be the centre of attention and is often truly theatrical, whether it be in a professional sense or merely in his private life. He is a born showman, generous to a fault and usually extremely creative. He can also be somewhat pompous, a little intolerant and, something which would often surprise all but his closest friends and family, very vulnerable. If yours is a Leonine character, the ideal stone for you to have as your own would be the tiger's eye.

Virgo: Meticulous – or fussy? Analytical – or a worrier? It depends upon which side of the Virgoan coin you look. No one works harder than the Virgo-type or has a more practical nature. Equally, no one so torments himself worrying about precision and detail. Although a Virgoan may appear aloof to some, if his natural reserve is broken down, he makes the most excellent of friends. If you are a Virgo-type, then the stone for you to wear is the green jasper or the sardonyx.

Libra: The Libra-type is charm personified. He loves beauty and harmony, both in his surroundings and in everyday life. He is romantic, inclined to idealism and cultured. He can also be frivolous and easily influenced by others – sometimes even gullible – preferring peace and harmony to following his own desires. Librans are often thought to be lazy but this is not necessarily so. There may be some indecision, but a Libran will often get what he wants – although sometimes in a rather roundabout way. Are you a Libra-type? Then your stone should be the sapphire.

Scorpio: The Scorpio subject has to work hard if he is to control the strength and intensity of his feelings rather than let them control him. He is passionate in all areas of life, whether we are talking about relationships, beliefs, work or upholding a cause. He can be persistent – or stubborn; imaginative – or suspicious; deeply loving – or unnecessarily jealous. A Scorpio-type makes the very best friend but often the very worst enemy, finding it hard ever to forgive a hurt. If yours is a Scorpio-type nature, your stone should be a ruby, an opal or a red jasper.

Sagittarius: The freedom-loving and optimistic Sagittarian can, on the other hand, be somewhat careless and irresponsible in his ways. He is sincere and frank – but may also appear to others to be tactless at times. He does not like the feeling of being tied down, whether by a boring job, a restrictive relationship or even the constriction of being in a small room. He will become restless and need to move on. If you are Sagittarian by nature, the stone you should wear is the topaz.

Capricorn: The careful, conventional Capricornian is someone on whom you can rely. He is determined and patient – and often needs to be. He can also be the complete pessimist, forecasting problems which will never arise. He is persistent and ambitious and will often have a delightful sense of humour – of the dry rather than the obvious type – but this will only be seen and understood by those closest to him. The stone which should be chosen by the Capricorn-type is the turquoise or the smokey quartz.

Aquarius: One person may consider the Aquarian to be delightfully unpredictable; another will call him an eccentric. Very few people really seem to get close to an Aquarius-type character and yet he is friendly and eager to lend a helping hand to all – although probably in a slightly detached way. He is often idealistic and interested in intellectual pursuits but he can also be perverse, delighting in an opinion merely because it is different to everyone else's. If you have an Aquarian character you will probably feel happiest wearing an amethyst.

Pisces: The sensitive, emotional Pisces-type is often very easily influenced by others. He is an escapist by nature. In a positive way this escapism can come to the fore as a talent for music, poetry or the theatre. If the influences are of a more negative sort, then the Piscean may try to escape through alcohol or drugs. The true Piscean is kind and sympathetic towards others but he may experience difficulty in the day-to-day running of his own life. If you feel that yours is a Piscean nature, you should balance this by wearing the gentle moonstone.

Section II
Crystals and Stones: their Meanings

1. Acquiring your own Stones

Choosing the stones you are to use for a psychic reading is an important task and not one to be undertaken in haste. At the end of this book you will find several names and addresses of firms and individuals who supply such stones. Many of them also have a mail order service and crystals for this purpose can be safely bought in this way, although I would not recommend it when purchasing crystals or stones for meditation or healing purposes. In that case you really need to see and handle the crystals for yourself as it is the individual crystal and not the type which is important. In the case of stones to be used for a reading, however, all stones of a similar type will have the same meaning and will be open to the same interpretation by the reader. For example, all red jaspers refer to strong emotions, whereas if you wanted a red jasper for healing purposes it would be better to see a selection of them in order to choose the one which felt right to you.

The number of stones you have in your possession is not, of itself, important; having a wide range of stones is what matters. I have in my own collection approximately one hundred and fifty stones but several are duplicated. In some cases, I even have five or six of one particular type. Quite often the value of having 'extra' stones of a particular variety is that it gives one a better idea of time and of intensity of a certain emotion. Later in this section you will find a list of what I consider to be the basic stones and crystals *essential* to a collection for the purpose of giving a reading but, if you feel that you would like to have more than one of any of the types listed, that can only make your task easier.

Once you have your own stones and crystals, wash them in clear running water and dry them well. You may have to do this quite often, once the stones are in regular use, as dust and regular handling can dull the colours and detract from the beauty of your treasures. One of the joys of working with crystals and stones is the pleasure one gets from looking at and handling the stones themselves, so be sure to keep them in pristine condition.

2. Meanings of Crystals and Stones in a Reading

The following are the crystals and stones which I consider to be essential if you want to be able to give a deep and comprehensive reading. As well as explaining the interpretations to you, I shall endeavour to point out how that interpretation can be varied according to the position of the individual stone and which stones are placed in close juxtaposition.

At no time should you forget that the stones are your 'vehicle', your 'focal point', and that you have to allow your own intuition or psychic ability to play a part in the reading too. However, as a starting point, the basic meanings of individual stones and crystals are given below.

For ease of identification, I suggest that you refer frequently to the photographs and the attached key while reading this section. It will enable you to become really well acquainted with the crystals and stones which are soon to become your means of divination.

You will see, for example, that the different varieties of agate have been separated to enable you to recognize them more easily. This is particularly important because, although each may be loosely classified under the one heading of 'agate', each type has its own special significance in the context of a reading.

Agate geode: The agate geode represents the potential psychic ability of the questioner. Obviously, this stone can be placed on the mat so that it shows the beauty of its interior – and this can vary in colour from palest lilac to a purple so deep that it is almost black – or it can be laid so that the rough, curved outside of the stone is uppermost.

Take note of how the questioner lays the stone. If the sparkling interior is uppermost, it means that he is either using his own psychic ability or at least that he is aware of its existence and would like to be able to develop it further. If the agate geode is placed face down upon the mat, the questioner's psychic or intuitive side is being blocked. It is for you to decide, taking note of the surrounding stones, whether this is a deliberate blocking of his own intuitive powers by someone who does not want to acknowledge their existence or whether outside circumstances are forcing that block upon him. For example, if he had recently suffered a bereavement or if he were in a state of depression or mental turmoil, the questioner's psychic ability would obviously be far less likely to function well.

Sometimes you will find that a particular person will turn the stone over in his hand several times before deciding to place it down one way or the other. This will often indicate that this is a time of the awakening of the questioner's own intuitive powers or perhaps that he is a little unsure of his own ability in this particular field.

It is important, therefore, that you do not just consider the stones as they lay upon the mat. It is necessary also to watch as they are selected. Sometimes you can learn a great deal from how a particular stone or crystal is handled before being either selected or rejected. So your task begins from the very moment that the questioner begins to look at the stones and crystals as they glitter before him.

Labradorite: The beautiful labradorite with its incandescent colours represents a place overseas.

Once again you have to consider the surrounding stones. Could the questioner be making a journey? Perhaps there is business to be done with a foreign country? If it were to be placed in close proximity to a deep red jasper, the presence of the labradorite could indicate that someone with whom the questioner is about to have a loving relationship actually comes from another country.

I have found that it is unusual for the labradorite to be merely an indication of a forthcoming holiday. There usually seems to be a deeper significance to its presence. If in fact it is a sign of a forthcoming vacation then there is some particular relevance to that trip. It could be that something particularly eventful will happen during the holiday; it could be that the holiday itself would only be possible should certain other events occur – and this, of course, would mean a great deal to the person actually having the reading.

Botswana agate: This beautifully streaked stone, resembling an old-fashioned sweetmeat, symbolizes some unexpected gift or pleasure.

As you can imagine, the precise meaning of this stone can vary considerably, ranging from something which is of vital importance, to a far more trivial treat. I have known it represent a pregnancy for one of my clients who had almost given up hope of ever having a child. I have also known it mean a surprise eightieth birthday party given for an elderly gentleman by his six grandchildren.

The only way in which you can come to a final decision upon the meaning of the Botswana agate is, once again, to look at the surrounding stones. These, as always, will give you a clear indication of the area which you should be considering.

There is, however, one additional point to note. Should the Botswana agate be selected when the questioner has a specific problem in mind rather than in the course of a general reading, then it is usually an indication of a happy solution to that problem – even if, at the time of the reading, that happy solution is seemingly improbable.

Aquamarine: The cool clear appearance of the aquamarine should serve to remind you of its interpretation. It is the stone of logic, of a clear mind, of common sense. It can also indicate that, although the questioner has come to consult you, he doubts the validity of any type of psychic reading and will believe those parts that he wishes to believe, rejecting the rest out of hand. This, however, is his problem rather than yours. Your task is to give an honest and forthright reading from the crystals and stones as you interpret them. If the questioner doubts what you have said as to the future, all you can do is to be firm in your views and tell him to wait and see. You will be amazed at how often these 'doubters' will contact you in the months to follow to apologize for ever having doubted you and to tell you how the events you foretold have come to pass.

Should you see an aquamarine in the midst of other stones showing turmoil and interference in the questioner's life, he may have temporarily lost sight of his own natural ability to think clearly and logically and to stand on his own two feet.

Iron Pyrite: The iron pyrite (also known simply as pyrite or pyrites) —otherwise known as 'Fool's Gold'—is a stone of which you should always take careful note. It is always of significance in a reading; its meaning is never trivial. It is a stone of mistrust, of deception or of folly. It indicates that all is not what it seems.

The interpretation when iron pyrite is present in any particular reading will naturally vary. It could mean that the questioner is liable to be deceived by a loved one, a business acquaintance or some other person. Once again, the area of deceit will be indicated by the surrounding stones. It could be a warning that a contemplated step should not be taken without careful consideration. It could, on the other hand, be a far more general indication that the questioner is a person who is perhaps a little too eager to place his trust in others unhesitatingly. This is often the case when you are reading for a person who is himself extremely trustworthy. Because of his own nature he tends not to realize that others may be a little more devious than he is himself.

At times the presence of the iron pyrite in a reading can be a sign of blind optimism on the part of the questioner – faith in the outcome of a specific situation rather than careful working towards the desired result. If you feel that this is the case, then it is for you to give a gentle warning that, although faith in oneself is an essential ingredient of success, nonetheless care and planning are often necessary too.

Although this stone may appear to have a 'doom and gloom' interpretation, the appearance of the iron pyrite in a reading should in fact be treated as a positive sign rather than a negative one. It is there as a signal, as a warning to the questioner that he should perhaps stop and think before rushing blindly on. It is not an indication of irrevocable destruction but is a fortuitous dose of preventative medicine.

Amethystine agate: You would do well to have two or more of these in your collection. I have four, of different sizes but each with an unmistakable grey and pink design.

The amethystine agate represents a forthcoming move of home and the reason for having more than one is so that you may be able to have some indication of time. The larger the stone, the more imminent the move. Obviously, should the amethystine agate be placed beside a labradorite, a move overseas could be possible in the not-too-distant future. If the nearest stone is one indicating a change of employment, perhaps that could be the reason for the move. Should the stone in closest proximity be one representing another person, however, it could be that it is that other person who will be the one to move rather than the questioner himself.

The amethystine agate you see in the photograph is the largest in my own collection. As I work on a two-year period within my readings, the largest stone represents to me either a move or at least a decision to move within the first six months of that period; the smallest stone would indicate that this is more likely within the last six months of that span, while the other two stones (not illustrated) would tell me that I am dealing with the interim period.

Tiger's eye: The tiger's eye can represent either independence or standing alone. Whether this appears to be a good or bad thing to the questioner depends upon whether that independence has been sought or has been forced upon him. For a businessman to form his own company, for example, or for a young man to leave home and branch out on his own, can be the most positive of steps. For someone to be made redundant or to be left alone when a marriage ends in divorce is far from a happy state of affairs. The tiger's eye can be an indication of any of the above as well as of other forms of independence. But, as it is the stone most closely associated in astrology with the sign of Leo, it is almost always a sign of a positive outcome. When the tiger's eye indicates independence – even if that independence has not been chosen – it is to be taken as a turning point and a change for the better – although it is quite possible that the questioner may in no way see it as such at the time.

Should more than one tiger's eye be present in the same reading, it usually indicates that the independence – whether in business or personal life – is in fact one of the most necessary factors in the questioner's life and that a great deal of what comes in the future hangs upon the way that he deals with the independence when it presents itself.

Petrified wood: Here is a positive indication of legal matters in the air – contracts, law suits and such.

Look carefully at the surrounding stones to see whether it is a case of an impending business contract – or possibly divorce proceedings. It could be a forthcoming conflict over a will – or a parking ticket! If the petrified wood is placed next to the iron pyrite, for example, it could mean that the questioner should have an innocent-looking contract or document closely examined by a legal expert in order to avoid future problems.

Quartz crystal: The quartz crystal is the symbol of energy, strength and vitality. It can indicate the return to good health of someone who has been feeling less than fit. It can be the taking charge of one's own life and finding the inner strength to do so successfully.

This is a strong, positive and hopeful sign for the future. It can mean that the questioner will succeed in some particular venture because of what he does for himself rather than because of outside influences.

Tektite: The dull black tektite is quite the opposite of the quartz crystal. It indicates hopelessness and despair and a tendency to give up. Although it appears in a particular reading, it may not always refer to the questioner himself. Quite often it will be an indication that someone in the questioner's life is in need of help and that that person may not be in a condition to do anything about it. So, in effect, it is telling the questioner that he is needed – sometimes to do something specific or sometimes just to be tolerant and understanding – possibly in a situation where he had hitherto not recognized the true facts.

If the tektite is surrounded by stones such as the quartz crystal and others of a vibrant and positive nature, it may indicate that the questioner himself has suffered a period of depression but that this is becoming a thing of the past and that the signs for the future are of strength and optimism.

Although it may appear that the tektite would give an ominous tone to the reading, I have always found that, whenever something less than happy appears, it is for a purpose. It is not just a portent of gloom but a means by which you can point out something in advance so that it may be handled well or even avoided altogether.

Dendritic agate: This is in fact one of those positive stones mentioned in the last section. The dendritic agate represents sunshine – either in its literal or symbolic sense. It could actually refer to some sunny place – when associated closely with the labradorite for example – perhaps giving some additional information concerning the location of a journey or a contact. It can also refer to the summer – the sunny part of the year – and this can be of assistance when trying to give the time when a particular event will occur.

However, the dendritic agate can also be taken symbolically. The solution to some problem concerning the questioner could turn out to be 'sunny' – that is, successful and pleasurable. The end of some stressful or disturbing period in his life could well be in

sight. If a direct question is asked and the dendritic agate is among
the stones chosen to provide the answer, then that answer is almost
certain to be positive.

Fluorite octahedron: There are good and bad aspects to this crystal –
as, of course, there are to most. The fluorite octahedron is
concerned with artistic ability and creativity – usually in a
practical and not merely an appreciative way. The presence of the
fluorite octahedron in a set of stones could well indicate a high
degree of artistic flair. We are not necessarily talking about
painting and drawing when we speak of art. It could just as easily
be music, writing, design or any other artistic form. But we are
definitely talking about a participant rather than an onlooker.

The positive aspect of the fluorite octahedron is that it indicates
a very high standard being achieved in the chosen art form so that,
whether it is the questioner's life's work or whether it is an
enjoyable pastime, success is extremely likely. The negative way
of looking at the same stone is that the questioner expects so much
of himself and is so self-demanding in his chosen artistic pursuit
that there is a danger that he will never be satisfied with whatever
he may create or – in extreme cases — that he will so doubt his
own talent and ability that he will refuse to try rather than allow
himself to fall short of his own expectations.

If the latter explanation seems to you to be the case, it may be
that a timely warning to the questioner is indicated. This refusal to
acknowledge any ability in one particular area of his life could
well be carried over into other areas too. Taken to the most
extreme of outcomes, it could result in a person who becomes
extremely introverted and who is unwilling to try anything at all
for fear of failure.

Serpentina: The serpentina is one of those stones which add to the
information to be gleaned from those around it rather than one
which gives information of itself. It often helps the reader to
differentiate between two or more people or things. For example,
if you wish to tell the questioner something about a young man,
possibly a son, he may say, 'But I have three sons.' If the serpentina
is there among the stones on the mat, it is there to tell you that you
are concerned with the eldest of the sons in question.

Similarly, if there are two possible romantic adventures ahead
of the questioner, the presence of the serpentina would indicate

that the one you are discussing concerns the person he has known for the greater length of time.

The nearest one can get to words describing what is represented by the presence of the serpentina in a reading is possibly 'oldest' or 'most mature'. It can, in addition, be of assistance when trying to determine a time of year, in that it also represents the summer period – say from June until early autumn.

Ruby: The ruby represents perfectionism. This can, of course, be a most laudable attribute, indicating a desire to do everything to the best of one's ability. It can also, however, result in one becoming over-strict, a hard taskmaster, either with regard to oneself or to others.

If you happen to be doing a reading for a student who is anxious about the results of examinations, the presence of the ruby would indicate a high standard – one with which that student should be delighted. If the questioner is a mother concerned over the prowess of a loved son or daughter, the ruby might well be trying to show that the mother is expecting more of the young person than he or she has the ability to give and is perhaps causing them stress or tension as a result. In very extreme cases the ruby can indicate a preoccupation with detail which is almost akin to fanaticism and it should be taken as a warning to the questioner to relax and be a little less hard on himself.

Purple agate: This is a sensitive stone, referring to the tender and emotional side of the questioner's nature. Looking at its presence in a positive way, particularly when it is teamed with stones indicating an artistic or a spiritual nature, the presence of the purple agate can serve only to enhance. If, however, it is among stones to do with business or legal matters, it may be a sign that the questioner should try and become a little more down-to-earth and pragmatic in these areas. The purple agate can, in other words, indicate either a sensitive or an over-sensitive nature.

There is another meaning to this stone and a more literal one. The purple agate also symbolizes water. Once again, look at the surrounding stones. Is there to be a move to a place which is near water – whether river, lake or sea? In this connection the presence of the purple agate is not likely to refer to a move *across* water, that is, overseas. That meaning, as we have seen and discussed earlier, would normally be indicated by the presence of a labradorite.

Jasper: Jaspers can be found in various shades ranging from a clear rich red to a deep dark green. Many are a mixture of the two, having a beautiful mottled appearance. In my own collection I also have a large jasper which is made up of the red and the green with streaks of deep mustard yellow. The meanings of these particular stones are linked very strongly with emotions deeply felt. It is important to take note of which particular shade of jasper the questioner chooses as the interpretation varies quite considerably.

Love, strong emotions, jealousy – even anger: these are the feelings indicated by the glowing presence of the red jasper. The greater the number of red jaspers present in a particular reading, the more his emotions are to the forefront of the questioner's mind – whether consciously or subconsciously. The red jasper will always mean that passionate feelings are involved – and those feelings will always be related to love. But remember that there are many kinds of love, not just the one-to-one romance. There is the love of parents for children and the love felt between close friends, as well as the love of one man and one woman. Quite apart from those examples, let us not forget the all-embracing love that can be felt for mankind in general.

What of the green jasper? Pity the one who has a predominance of green jaspers among his stones for there is the rejected lover, the unsuccessful suitor or perhaps the parent ignored by an uncaring child. Of course, it is for the reader to decide whether these emotions reflect an actual situation or whether they are the fears in the mind of the questioner. Could it be that he fears rejection and that this is making him faint-hearted? Perhaps the over-protective parent is failing to recognize the quest for freedom of the child who is no longer a child. The emotions, of course, are just as deeply felt even when they are mistaken. The larger the proportion of green jaspers to red, the greater the presence of the negativity in the mind of the questioner. A stone almost wholly green could be a sign that he has almost given up in despair, whereas one that is red with just a few flecks of green would show that he is able to keep most of his negative thoughts under control.

The jasper which contains all three colours – the red, the green and the yellow – is a sign of anxiety in relation to love and relationships. It tends to be chosen by someone whose emotional experiences in the past have ended unhappily and who for that reason feels unsure about the possibility of any new relationship. Often you will find that this questioner has erected mental barriers around himself as a form of protection against future emotional pain. In many cases, of course, these mental barriers, if unrecognized, may actually prevent the successful development of a relationship, serving to increase and to perpetuate the negative feelings. I always feel that the presence of this particular multi-coloured jasper in a group of stones is a good thing in that it may lead the reader to point out the harm that these negative feelings are doing and to bring to an end this vicious circle of self-doubt.

Amethyst: The amethyst, with its deep mauve beauty, is truly a spiritual crystal. Its presence in a reading is an indication of a strong interest or ability in spiritual matters. It is not unusual to find several amethysts in one reading; after all, a person with spiritual feelings and beliefs is quite likely to be affected by those feelings and beliefs in several areas of his life.

As in so many of the other cases we have discussed, it is important to take note of the other stones placed in close proximity to the amethyst. Do you see an aquamarine? This could well be a sign that the questioner could be a teacher or a leader in some spiritual field. Is there perhaps a rose quartz nearby indicating strong healing abilities? Or an agate geode showing that the questioner leans towards clairvoyance or mediumship?

As well as the amethyst itself, there is the eight-sided amethystine octahedron. This, too, is an indication of spiritual beliefs and aptitudes but in a somewhat less beneficial way. The amethystine octahedron will often be selected by one who finds it difficult to keep his feet on the ground and who leans so strongly towards the spiritual that he becomes unrealistic in the running of his everyday life. Whether he is someone who is inclined blindly to follow the words of some guru thousands of miles away or whether he sees his fellow man (and, indeed, the world) through idealistic eyes, he is likely to have problems coping with day-to-day living and particularly with human relationships.

Light green jasper: This stone is far less common than the dark green variety discussed a little earlier in this section. It is a glorious golden-green without a hint of red and just to look at it is to know its meaning – sheer joy and happiness. Not for this stone the calm tranquillity of contentment; here is the absolute delight which comes when 'all's right with the world'.

One usually finds that the light green jasper is selected when a question has been asked – and it is obviously to be taken as a sign that the questioner will be more than pleased with the outcome of a particular situation.

Turquoise: The turquoise indicates a feeling of peace and contentment. It may not be as vibrant and effervescent as the light green jasper but it is somehow deeper and certainly much less transient. No one can hope to maintain the feeling of 'clap hands and jump for joy' of the light green jasper but how sought-after and enviable is a long-lasting state of contentment and calm pleasure.

There are two ways in which the turquoise can be chosen. It could be one of the original nine stones selected or it could be picked when a question has been asked. If the former is the case, this would tell you quite a considerable amount about the personality of the questioner. If the latter, then, once again, you have an almost certain sign that the answer to the question will be in the affirmative.

White and amber agate: The presence of a white agate surrounded with an amber border informs the reader that books and the written word have a special significance here. The questioner could well be either an actual or 'would-be' writer. He could be undertaking a course of study – or he could be the teacher. Look at the surrounding stones. The aquamarine placed close to the white and amber agate would tell you that studying is likely to be the case. The proximity of the rutilated quartz – an almost certain sign of artistic ability – would be likely to indicate writing in its more creative form, whether poetry or prose. Add to those a money-stone (of which more later in this section) and you have writing as a possible source of income. Do not forget to use your intuition during an interpretation. Remember that one can also write music – and that accountants write figures in books! The real significance of this, as of each stone, is for you to identify, taking into account the other stones selected.

Moss agate: The moss agate is a beautiful stone to find in a reading. It signifies peace of mind and the ending of a period of anxiety. Sometimes the questioner will choose several moss agates among his stones and this is often a sign that he is in fact searching for peace of mind and that it is well within his grasp if only he could stop searching so hard and take the time to look within himself.

I always find it a particular pleasure when a questioner whose reading has contained several of those stones showing a distressed state of mind comes to see me again after an interval of time and I watch him pick one or more of the moss agates in place of the stones previously chosen. I know then that things are beginning to improve and that the atmosphere is much more positive than it had previously been.

Rutilated quartz: This clear honey-coloured crystal has running through it what look like threads of pure gold. Its presence in a reading is a sign of artistic ability on the part of the person who has selected it. This ability may or may not be recognized by the questioner himself; he may be putting it to some use or choosing to ignore it. The talent may lie in any creative form – music, painting, design, etc. – although the rutilated quartz does not usually apply to creative writing. This is far more likely to be indicated by the presence of the white and amber agate as we have already seen. Obviously, if the rutilated quartz is placed close to a stone representing finance, it is probable that the questioner either does, or at some time in the future will, use his artistic ability to make money.

Sometimes a questioner will insist that he has no creative ability at all – that he never has had and never will. In such cases you will almost always find that what the stones are saying is that some form of artistic outlet would be beneficial to him. Perhaps he is going through a tense and anxious period in his life. Perhaps he is finding it difficult to express his emotions as easily as he would wish. Possibly he is working very hard and forgetting the old adage about all work and no play making 'Jack a dull boy'. Whatever the circumstances, it would appear that he could be helped by finding an outlet which is more creative and recreational.

Agate with fossils: This rather dull-looking little stone is in fact an indication of good fortune. Its meaning is simple; it concerns money and it is always a sign of an increase rather than a loss. Of course, just how that increase is to come about could be in any of a number of ways. If you should see a turritella agate nearby, you will know that a change of job is imminent. If there is a piece of petrified wood in close proximity, the money is likely to come as the result of a legal matter of some sort. The Botswana agate would indicate a gift or perhaps a win.

Rose quartz: The lovely rose quartz is the healer's crystal. Its presence in a reading is a certain indication that the questioner has healing abilities, whether or not he chooses to make use of them. However, do not fall into the trap of thinking in terms only of spiritual healing. A nurse is a healer as is a dental surgeon. Healing may be of the mind or of the body and, particularly if there is an aquamarine close to the rose quartz for example, there could be signs that the questioner would make an excellent counsellor or therapist – healing minds and emotions rather than healing physical ailments. It is only when one sees the rose quartz surrounded by stones such as the amethyst which refer to the spiritual side of life that the meaning is spiritual healing.

If the rose quartz does not appear in the original stones and crystals chosen by the questioner but can be seen among those chosen when a question about a particular person has been asked, it would indicate that the person about whom information has been sought could well be in need of healing of some sort, whether physical, mental or emotional.

Citrine quartz: The citrine quartz is a beautiful crystal with its barley-sugar-coloured citrine at one end and the frosty white of a quartz crystal at the other. It is the crystal of new beginnings. Sometimes these new beginnings are actual, such as a change of employment, a new venture, a hitherto unpursued interest. At other times there seems to be a search, a need for something more in the life of the questioner.

The new beginnings whose presence is indicated by this crystal are usually those which come unbidden to the questioner. An opportunity for a new job, a new home or even a new relationship which appears to be handed to him 'on a plate'. A door which seems to be opened before him rather than one on which he has to bang. It is far less likely to be something which he has actually made some deliberate attempt to seek out.

Blue lace agate: Quite simply, the lovely and delicate blue lace agate indicates the presence of a girl – often a daughter. Now this is one of those stones whose presence in the reading is very strongly coloured by the types of crystal or stone around it. Should it appear close to a dark-green jasper, for example, then there would seem to be some concern or anxiety to do with the young girl. If the questioner says: 'But I have three daughters,' you will usually find that there is one in particular who has been on his mind for a specific reason just lately. Perhaps the daughter has been suffering from ill health; perhaps she has been going through some emotional upset of her own which has caused worry to her parent; or perhaps it is something as straightforward as the awaited outcome of an examination or the result of an interview. Whichever is the case, look around the blue lace agate to judge the positivity or negativity of the outcome of the particular situation.

It may be that the girl or young woman concerned is not in fact related to the questioner at all but she would always be a person who is close in some way and not merely the child of a neighbour or a casual acquaintance.

If the blue lace agate appears to be isolated in the reading and you cannot connect any of the surrounding stones with it, then you should ask the questioner to concentrate on the person in mind and to choose three further stones and put them on the mat near to the blue lace agate. This should serve to enlighten you as to the significance of the presence of the stone in this particular reading.

Agate quartz: The blue lace agate is an indication of a daughter or a young girl and, in just the same way, the agate quartz represents a son or a young man. Once again, it is necessary to concentrate on the surrounding stones and crystals fully to understand the reason and the explanation for the presence of the agate quartz in the reading. Sometimes it will become obvious that there has been some sort of friction or disappointment between the questioner and the young man concerned and, depending upon the stones and crystals in close proximity, you should be able to glean some information as to the outcome of the situation and how long it is likely to continue.

Bloodstone: The bloodstone is an indication of physical aches and pains or illness. It does not of necessity denote anything seriously wrong with the questioner or anyone who is close to him. Depending upon where in the reading the stone appears, the bloodstone could be a sign of a past illness, or something troubling the questioner now or it could be a warning to him to slow down a little. It is never a 'prophet of doom'. If any stone which could be classed as 'negative' appears in a reading, you will always find that it is there because a realization of its presence will be a gentle reminder to the questioner to take care, and not because it is an indication of coming disaster. Obviously it is important to point this out so as not to send him away in a negative frame of mind. Sometimes, of course, the bloodstone will be placed close to a stone indicating another person and, in that case, the aches or pains would be in relation to that particular person and not to the questioner himself.

I have quite often found when doing a reading that, although the pain or discomfort indicated may have a physical manifestation, the presence of the bloodstone is more likely to be an indication of the stress and tension which is causing the pain and that a gentle word to the questioner as to methods of overcoming the problems of tension in his everyday life is what is really needed.

Pink/grey jasper: We have already seen how the blue lace agate symbolizes a young girl or daughter and the agate quartz denotes the presence of a young man or a son. In just the same way, the pale pink jasper with the grey edges signifies the presence of an older person – usually a parent or someone who has stood in the place of a parent. By 'older' I do not mean one who is the senior of the questioner by just a few years but someone who is considerably advanced in age.

The presence of this stone would indicate that a situation around or concerning the older person is going to have some effect upon the immediate future of the questioner. It could be that a parent will be moving either nearer or further away. It could be a gift which is to be received from the elderly lady or gentleman. The main point to note is that it is bound to have some influence upon the future plans or aspirations of the person to whom you are giving the reading.

Turritella agate: The turritella agate with its mottled design is an indication of a change in the work situation of the questioner. It could be something as simple as a change from one job to another; it could be a promotion within the job that he has now. Obviously, should the turritella agate be placed close to the 'money stone', then that change, whether small or large, is bound to be beneficial financially.

If you see a labradorite close by, the change of work is likely to be concerned with another country. Sometimes this could mean that the questioner is actually going to work abroad but it could also refer to the fact that the company or firm for whom the questioner is going to work is a foreign company. Should a tiger's eye be placed next to the turritella agate, then it is likely that the questioner is going to work for himself – and if the golden dendritic agate happens to be nearby, he can know that he is taking a step very much in the right direction from the point of view of personal satisfaction as well as materially.

Now you have been introduced to the basic stones and crystals necessary to give a reading. Before you can go further you need to get to know your own stones and crystals really well so that not only do you recognize each one instantly, but, by taking in at a glance all the stones and crystals on the mat, you are able to assess a situation and therefore to give as much help as possible to the person who has come to consult you.

3. Reading from Crystals and Stones

Once you have your own crystals and stones, you will naturally be anxious to set about using them. Before you do, be sure to spend plenty of time getting to know them. You must treat each one as a trusted friend, must be able to recognize it instantly and must be very sure of its meaning. It is important to realize that, as we have seen, each individual crystal or stone has a very different meaning – just as each tarot card has a different meaning. Some will be similar – there are several 'emotional' stones, for example, but the degree or intensity of the meaning may vary. In addition the reading is, of course, greatly affected by the selection of a number of stones of a similar type, or by the placing of certain stones in close juxtaposition.

Obviously you will have to find what is for you the most comfortable way of doing a reading. What I propose to do here is to tell you how I go about it but remember that you are an individual and must change or adapt the method to suit yourself.

When I give a reading the questioner sits opposite me at a table. Between us is a tray covered with black velvet on which are placed the stones and crystals. Before the questioner is a mat – also of black velvet. I prefer to use that particular fabric as I feel that it shows the stones and crystals in all their beauty. Look in the window of any jeweller's shop and you will see displays of precious gems set out on dark-coloured velvet. (And what are we working with, you and I, but the precious gems of nature?) The fact that the cloth is black also helps to focus attention on the crystals and stones themselves and to avoid surrounding distractions.

I ask the questioner to choose nine stones, to search among them, taking as much time as may be necessary, for those which he finds most attractive – selecting them by appearance rather than by 'feel'. Those nine stones are then placed upon the black velvet mat, either at random (if there is such a thing) or in whatever grouping or pattern the questioner may choose. It is from these nine crystals and stones that I begin my reading.

'Look at the crystals and stones in the tray. Run your fingers through them. Then select the nine which most appeal to you.' This is the way a typical reading begins. Sometimes the questioner is decisive and chooses a selection of crystals and stones without pause. At other times the choice may be slow and laboured, with several changes of mind. But, whichever is the case, this 'selection time' is by no means an idle period for the reader. It is a time to watch carefully to see which stones are being handled and inspected before being rejected and to notice which are discarded when a final substitution is made.

It is interesting, too, and very relevant, to see in which order crystals and stones are chosen. The first ones to be selected will tell you what is uppermost in the mind of the questioner. Suppose he reaches immediately for a golden brown tiger's eye. As you know, this represents some form of independence. Watch closely. Is this followed by a speckled turritella agate, indicating to you that he is likely to become more independent in his working life? Perhaps he is thinking of starting his own business. If a red jasper is selected just after the tiger's eye, it would tell you that his independence problems are likely to be connected with his emotional life. Whereas, should the second stone chosen be a pink agate, it is far more likely to be the case that he has difficulty in breaking free from a possessive parent.

Sometimes the questioner will select the first five or six stones quickly and decisively and then appear to have difficulty in choosing the last few. Take note of this for it tells you that there is really only one major problem on his mind – one area about which he is unsure – and that he feels quite able to cope adequately with the rest of his life.

People vary greatly in the manner in which they actually place the crystals and stones upon the mat. Some will just toss them down haphazardly with no real thought for their arrangement. It is those people who tend to have the greatest difficulty in putting their own life in order and who would like someone else to do it for them. 'Here you are,' they are saying. 'Here is my mess. You sort it out.' It is not a bad thing, once you have mentally taken note of the situation, to ask this questioner to separate the crystals and stones from one another so that you may read them more easily. Although he may appear diffident about doing it, it is actually of great benefit to him to be put in a position where he has to make some order out of chaos.

There are others who, even after they have selected their nine crystals and stones, seem to take for ever to arrange them on the mat. They make neat symmetrical little patterns and spend ages moving the stones around until they are satisfied with their design. These people are usually fearful of life and very unsure of themselves. They are lacking in confidence and do not usually have a true sense of their own worth.

So you see, to the reader, the time taken by the questioner in selecting and arranging his crystals and stones is of vital importance. Before you even begin to study and talk about the stones on the mat, you will know several things about the questioner and his personality.

Those crystals and stones which were discarded when the selection was being made also have a significance all of their own. Any which are picked up and examined before being rejected relate to situations which have recently passed out of the questioner's life; perhaps a problem which has now been solved; or perhaps a trait or characteristic of the questioner's personality which either circumstances or personal efforts have succeeded in altering. Any crystal or stone which, at the last moment is set aside so that another can take its place is telling you something too. It is indicating an aura of change surrounding the questioner at the present time. For example if, at the last moment, the dark green agate of anxiety is discarded in favour of the small turquoise of contentment, it is a certain indication of a change in the mental outlook of the questioner himself. It is up to the reader – if the matter is to be pursued as important – to discover the whys and wherefores of that change, often by reference to the stones surrounding the one finally selected.

I have found that the crystals and stones are especially adept at conveying emotions to the reader. Most forms of divination can indicate facts and events – and indeed the stones can too – but few forms seem as well-suited to transmitting thoughts and feelings, both those of the questioner and those of anyone to whom he is particularly attached or about whom he has recently been thinking.

It is important, of course, to make the questioner feel confident and to reassure him that you are genuinely receiving information through the crystals and stones. For this reason it is a good thing to begin by speaking briefly about the past and the present. This naturally gives more credibility to anything you say about the future. You cannot offer proof of what you say about events which have not yet taken place, but if you have been able to describe with accuracy feelings and events in the questioner's immediate past, as well as those surrounding him at the present time and of which he is aware, he is far more likely to have faith in what you tell him about his future.

Having done that, it is time to turn your attention to the crystals and stones in front of you. Is there a predominance of any one particular type? If there is, this indicates that the questioner's mind is occupied to a great extent with one particular problem. Suppose, for example, that among the nine crystals and stones selected, five or six of them are deep red jaspers. You would know that the questioner is thinking predominantly about love and relationships. Look at those jaspers. Are they placed close together in one area? Are there perhaps two entirely separate groups? Which is the larger?

What do the answers to these questions tell you? Let us suppose that there are two entirely separate groups of jaspers. This would indicate a situation where there are two entirely separate relationships around the questioner. Look at the stones themselves. Do the ones which are speckled with dark green tend to be in one group, while the other group consists of jaspers of a more even red? This would tell you that the problems are arising in regard to one of the relationships in particular. (Remember, of course, that you may well be dealing with desires and emotions within the questioner himself rather than with an actual situation. It may be something which he wishes would develop rather than something which already has.) Take things one step further and consider the crystals and stones around the 'problem area'. If your questioner is a woman and there is a stone indicating the presence of another woman, could that be a problem? If the labradorite, the stone of long-distance travel, is nearby, perhaps the questioner is separated, either temporarily or permanently, from a loved one. If there is a piece of petrified wood indicating legal matters in the vicinity of those speckled jaspers, it could be that divorce is in the air. It is for you to judge, taking into consideration both the principal groups of crystals and stones and those immediately surrounding them.

Let us take another example. You know already that the beautiful pink and grey amethystine agate denotes a change of environment. In most instances you can interpret this quite literally as a move of home. It is quite a good idea to have two or three of these stones of differing sizes in your collection as this can often help to give you an indication of time. For example, in my own collection of crystals and stones, I have four amethystine agates, all equally lovely but of four very different sizes. I know that, should the questioner pick the largest of these, then the move of home is in the comparatively near future. It becomes further away in time as the stones decrease in size. I tend to work on the basis that a reading covers approximately a two-year period so the smallest amethystine agate will indicate a move of home towards the end of that time.

Once again, consider the surrounding crystals and stones. Do you see the labradorite of long-distance travel? Is there perhaps a purple agate indicating that the move is likely to be to a place near water, whether a river or the sea? Is the turritella agate, the stone representing a change of employment, very close to the original stone, showing you a possible reason for the move? All these things are relevant and will help you to add meat to the bare bones of the reading.

What do these examples tell us? They show us that it is not merely the meaning of an individual crystal or stone which is important, but its position on the mat and which other stones are to be found in close proximity.

Once you have dealt with the more obviously important aspects of the reading, it is time to move on and consider the remainder of the nine crystals and stones selected. Look at each in turn and decide whether it stands alone or should be linked in the reading with one or more of the stones closest to it.

It may be that there is some point about which you feel uncertain in your own mind and which you feel could be of some importance when developed. The best way to deal with this is to ask the questioner to focus his attention for a moment on the stones which first gave you this feeling and then to select three or more stones from those in the tray, placing them on the mat. The three extra crystals or stones chosen will give you the information you require.

Let us take an example. Suppose the questioner had put on the mat a dark green bloodstone. Now, as you already know, this can either mean some kind of physical pain, such as backache or migraine, or it can have something to do with feelings of worry or anxiety. You may feel the need to develop that point, but if the bloodstone stands apart from the other crystals and stones on the mat it may be difficult to do so. Once the questioner has chosen three additional stones, however, things should be much clearer. Suppose he selects crystals and stones which represent younger people, for example – such as the blue lace agate or the agate quartz. It could be that he is concerned about one or more of his children. And if another happens to be the white and amber agate which, as you know, is indicative of books and learning, perhaps the concern is to do with their academic life – examinations could be approaching. If he chooses instead the turritella agate which denotes a change of work, that could be the reason for his anxiety.

It is essential to remember in this context that the problem need not be one concerning the questioner personally. It could well be that someone to whom he is attached has a worry and that the questioner, because of his close link with that person, is picking up that worry. If that is the case, it will become clear when the three extra crystals or stones are selected.

Once you have dealt with all the crystals and stones on the mat, it is wise to ask the questioner whether he has any particular problem or any area of his life about which he would like to know more. If the answer is yes, you must remove all the crystals and stones from the mat, placing them to one side but *not* returning them to the tray. Then ask the questioner to indicate the area about which he is curious – although you do not want him to give you too much information. Tell him to focus his mind upon that question and, at the same time, to select a further five crystals or stones. These are then placed on the mat for you to consider, bearing in mind the aspect of his life which the questioner has mentioned to you.

Suppose the questioner says to you: 'I should like to know more about my spiritual development.' Depending upon the five crystals and stones selected, you should be able to help him. If he picks one or more pieces of rose quartz – the healing stone – it might be that he will develop as a healer. The agate geode would indicate a clairvoyant ability although, as we have already seen, if this is placed face down upon the mat, it indicates that, whether deliberately or subconsciously, he is blocking that ability himself. If he selects the cubic golden iron pyrite he might well have to take care that he does not become too gullible – perhaps becoming so anxious for rapid spiritual development that he is tempted to follow blindly some particular sect or guru. Whatever are the five crystals or stones selected when the questioner is concentrating upon one particular aspect of his life, do not doubt that they will give you the help you need to answer and advise.

To help you to understand even more clearly how to give a psychic reading using crystals and semiprecious stones, in the next section you will find several examples of actual readings that I have given in the past – although naturally the clients' names have been changed.

Section III
Readings from Crystals and Stones

1. James

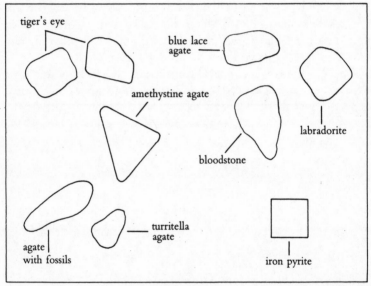

Figure 1

James has been a regular client of mine for some time. When he first came to see me in late 1983 he was in his late forties, a large and somewhat silent man. He sat at the table and, almost immediately, picked out the five stones in the group on the left, banging them down quite firmly on the mat. Then, after some hesitation, he picked up the cubic piece of iron pyrite (fool's gold). He held it for a few moments, turning it over in his hand, before discarding it. Then, with rather more thought than before, he sifted through the crystals and stones in the tray, finally selecting the three in the top right hand of the diagram – the bloodstone, the blue lace agate and the labradorite.

One more to choose. This time James really seemed to be having difficulty. He picked up several different crystals and stones only to replace them in the tray. At length, almost as though he could not resist it, he returned to the piece of iron pyrite, placing it in solitary splendour in the front right-hand corner of the mat. With a sigh he sat back and looked at me in anticipation.

Let us look at the left-hand group first and see what we have. First to be selected were the two pieces of tiger's eye which, as we know, concern independence of some sort. The other three – the turritella agate, the amethystine agate and the dark agate encrusted with fossils – followed in fairly quick succession. As there were two pieces of tiger's eye and as James was so definite in his placing of them, I felt that this indicated something to do with feelings of personal independence and that concern in that area was uppermost in his mind. Before I even mentioned this to James, however, I looked at the surrounding stones to see what information they could give me. There were no jaspers there – nothing to indicate that relationships or love were involved – so James did not appear to be approaching a breakdown in his marriage. What I did see was a turritella agate which symbolizes some sort of change in his work and a fossilized agate or 'money stone'. Putting all these together, I told James that I thought that there would be a change in his work situation and that, if he was not already working for himself, it was likely that he soon would be and that this would be a financially profitable step for him to take.

James responded by telling me that this had been a desire of his for some time and that he had made all the necessary plans and enquiries but that he was anxious as to whether, by taking this step, he would be jeopardizing the financial security of his family. The stones, as you can see, indicated that not only would the venture be financially viable but – because of the presence of *two* pieces of tiger's eye – he would not be forced to lose that independence once he had gained it. This delighted him as the thought of being 'his own man' was, if anything, more important to him than the increase in money.

The fifth stone in that group was the amethystine agate,

symbolizing a move of home. Not only that, but it was the largest of these stones in my collection, telling me that the move was likely to be in the comparatively near future. Because it had been placed alongside the other stones we have just been looking at, I felt that the move might well be connected in some way with the new business. James told me that he certainly had no plans to move at that time, although naturally the family would like a larger house should this be possible at some future date. He did not think, as I suggested, that any move was likely to take place within a year.

I then turned to the group of crystals and stones in the top right of the diagram. That group consisted of a blue lace agate, a bloodstone and a piece of labradorite. The first of these, as you already know, usually represents a young woman, sometimes a daughter. The bloodstone is a symbol of pain or distress and the labradorite indicated to me that the problem had to do with overseas.

I wanted to be clearer in my mind about this particular group of stones, so I asked James to focus his attention on them and to pick one more stone from those in the tray. After just a moment of hesitation, he chose a rather large jasper, heavily marked with green and gold, which as you know, depicts a problem in the area of relationships.

I explained the meaning of these stones to James and he told me that he had, in fact, a daughter living in the United States and that he had been feeling a little anxious about her of late – although he could not put a finger on the reason for this anxiety. I felt that his daughter was perhaps in some sort of emotional turmoil and that James would hear about it within a very short time.

I then turned my attention to the piece of iron pyrite which James had placed – quite apart from all the others – at the front right-hand corner of the mat. I was puzzled because James did not appear to be the sort of man to do anything without good reason and yet, as he freely admitted, he had felt compelled to select the iron pyrite even though it did not really appeal to him as a stone.

As you will have learned from the previous section, iron pyrite indicates an area where trust may be misplaced. James had shown obvious reluctance in picking this stone and I suggested that he instinctively doubted someone around him but was unwilling to admit this fact, even to himself. James informed me that he had been considering taking someone into his business venture as a second-in-command. Logic told him that this man would be an excellent co-worker, yet some deep instinct which he could not explain seemed to be holding him back.

I never in the course of my readings tell the questioner what he should or should not do. That is not my job. I prefer to point out the possibilities and to indicate those areas where caution might be advisable. In this case I suggested to James that he should weigh up the pros and cons of this proposed business relationship very carefully indeed before proceeding.

Some six months after the initial visit James came to see me once more. He told me that he had gone ahead with the business venture he had been considering and that this seemed to have been a wise move as, even though these were early days, he was more than keeping his head above water and prospects for the future seemed bright.

The only fly in the ointment had been difficulties arising because he had suppressed his own instincts and had in fact employed the very person about whom he had felt so doubtful. This man had turned out to be less than scrupulous in his business methods and James had been fortunate to have discovered that fact before allowing him to become more deeply involved in the enterprise.

With regard to his anxiety about his daughter, James had discovered that her relationship with her fiancé had been going through a bad phase at the time he had come to me for a reading. Happily, the latest telephone call from America had reassured him that all was now well. The young couple were together again and in fact, as James told me with obvious parental joy, a wedding was to take place in the very near future.

As he was about to leave, almost as an afterthought, James turned to me and told me that he and his wife had begun looking at houses in a nearby area and were hoping to move within the next few months.

Now you have some idea of how a reading from crystals and stones works. The following are a few more examples so that you may understand it even more clearly and be better able to conduct a reading yourself.

2. Marianne

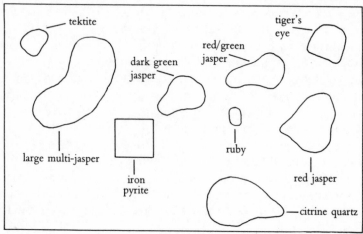

Figure 2

Marianne was a tall, attractive young woman of 28. She was a smartly dressed businesswoman with, as it turned out, a deceptively calm and self-assured manner. She sat down and began to select her crystals and stones immediately.

First came the tektite in the top left-hand corner of the diagram. This was followed almost at once by the iron pyrite in the centre and then the tiger's eye in the top right. Then there was a pause while Marianne rummaged around among the crystals and stones in the tray, picking up first one and then another and discarding each in turn. Suddenly, and in quick succession, she selected the four assorted jaspers and placed them on the mat. A little more thoughtfully she picked out the small mauve ruby and added it to the group of jaspers on the right. Then she stopped. 'You have only chosen eight,' I pointed out. 'There are no others that I like,' she replied. I assured her that it was essential to have nine stones on the mat before I would commence the reading and, rather reluctantly, she finally picked up the citrine quartz and placed it, on its own, in the right-hand corner of the mat. Then she sat back and looked at me expectantly.

As you look at the diagram showing you the crystals and stones chosen, you will notice that each one is concerned very much with emotions, relationships and feelings. Nothing that she had selected gave any indication that Marianne had any great problems surrounding her which were connected with her professional or practical life. Let us now consider the individual crystals and stones one by one.

The fact that the first stone to be chosen was the piece of black tektite is concerned with depression, anxiety or discontent. By choosing this stone first, Marianne had shown that this was a very strong feeling within her at that moment – whatever her calm outward appearance. The presence of tektite in a reading is never a very good sign. It is not in itself a portent of unfortunate events to come but it does show that the questioner has an inner – and sometimes illogical – anxiety to do with one particular area of his or her life and it is this feeling of anxiety or negativity which is sometimes so difficult to shift.

I looked then at the second stone which Marianne had chosen. This was quite a large piece of golden tiger's eye. Now the tiger's eye can have a good, strong positive feeling of independence to it – a feeling of being able to stand on one's own two feet. But the reverse of this coin – and the most common meaning when the tiger's eye appears surrounded by emotional stones such as the jaspers – is a feeling of being alone, isolated and unwanted. It is often seen in this way when we are dealing with someone who has suffered either a divorce or a bereavement. Perhaps this was so in Marianne's case. Before speaking, I considered the stones around the tektite and the tiger's eye.

Beside the unhappy tektite was the large red, green and yellow jasper – the stone which tells of deep, emotional hurt – and hurt which has had a long-lasting effect. It is also the stone of emotional turmoil and uncertainty. I told Marianne that I felt that she had been deeply hurt in the past and that this had caused a lowering of her own self-image. Now to say that someone has been hurt emotionally is not in itself conclusive; very few people reach adulthood without suffering some sort of pain because of relationships. But in Marianne's case I felt that this was something far deeper and not just the failure of a love affair. The impression I had was of a feeling of total rejection which had been allowed to colour her whole life.

Marianne told me that when she was ten years old her father had left his wife and only child to live with another woman. Although as an adult woman she could now well understand that marriages fail and husbands and wives part, the 10-year-old little girl had felt totally and utterly rejected by the father she had adored. Because she had had no inkling of her parents' separation until it actually happened, she had since that time been somewhat wary of men in general and of the permanence of seemingly happy relationships in particular.

This fact was borne out by the selection of jaspers surrounding the tiger's eye. There was the dark green jasper of worry and anxiety, the red and green jasper which denotes sadness and disappointment in a loving relationship and the deep red jasper usually selected by someone with a deep loving nature – one who longs to give and receive love. Nestling among them was a small ruby telling me that Marianne was extremely self-critical in this area of her life and was very hard on herself, probably taking all the blame for any relationships which failed.

In addition to the stones already mentioned, right in the centre of the mat stood a shiny golden cube of iron pyrite. As you know, the iron pyrite can be a sign of mistrust or of gullibility. I felt that the message here was twofold. Firstly, that Marianne was not very good at choosing the men in her life. She was so desperately crying out for love and affection that she was often fooled by any man who seemed to offer her what she was seeking. Naturally, since this type of relationship was doomed to failure almost before it began, when it did in fact break down, that event only served to increase her own feelings of inadequacy in this respect. She was on an emotional downward spiral, trapped in a vicious circle from which she did not seem able to escape.

The other point indicated by the presence of the iron pyrite – especially when placed right in the centre – was that, even if the right man did come along for her, she would feel unable to trust in that relationship. And, of course, in time the man concerned would become aware of that mistrust and would resent it – and thus would begin yet another vicious circle doomed to end in the failure of yet another relationship.

I put these points to Marianne who agreed, although with some reservations. She did, indeed, feel that she was often drawn towards the wrong type of man. She had had several brief relationships in her life and had been almost relieved when they had come to an end. On the two occasions when she had become involved with what she considered to be a really worthwhile man, she had herself ruined the relationship by becoming jealous and suspicious without having been given any reason to be so. What was happening was that she had such a low opinion of herself in this area of her life that she could never believe that any man could possibly want to remain faithful and true to her.

What Marianne really wanted to know was whether she could ever get off this treadmill of infatuation, jealousy and separation which had become her emotional pattern of life. At this point I turned to the last remaining crystal – the pretty citrine quartz standing all alone in one corner of the mat.

I felt it was quite significant that this was the one crystal Marianne had had difficulty in selecting. All the others had been picked quite quickly and easily – although not necessarily happily. When it came to the citrine quartz, however, Marianne had thought long and hard before finally choosing it. And yet this was the one symbol of hope in her emotional future.

The citrine quartz, you will remember, is the sign of new beginnings. Often when it is selected in a reading it refers to the working life of the questioner. In this case, however, the only aspect of Marianne's life to feature at all was that of her emotions and her relationships and so I felt that it was in this area that there would be a new beginning. I did not feel that the new beginning would necessarily take the shape of a new man in her life – there was no stone to indicate this – but that it was the start of a new understanding of herself and therefore a new outlook on partnerships and love. The fact that Marianne had had some trouble and had had almost to force herself to select that particular crystal indicated to me that, although her unconscious mind recognized that this new understanding was around the corner, she was still somewhat afraid of facing the truth about herself and her emotions.

Marianne and I spent quite a long time discussing the reading and what it had shown. She did not accept very readily that there would be a change in her attitude and response to men but she did agree that I had given her food for thought. It was the first time that she had realized how great had been the effect of her father's departure from the family home all those years ago. This in itself was a good starting point and, because Marianne was an obviously intelligent and deep-thinking young woman, I had little doubt that she would begin to see how she had, in fact, been her own worst enemy when it came to coping with her emotional life.

Let us pause here to consider the value of a reading, whether from crystals, stones or any other medium. Sometimes the value to a questioner is not what you are able to tell them in comparatively definite terms about future events; sometimes what is needed is to point out a situation which is around them and from which it is within their own power to extricate themselves. To be able to do this and to send someone off with a new way of thinking and a feeling of positive hope for the future must be the most rewarding achievement for any reader.

To return to Marianne, having covered the subject of her emotional life – and this was obviously the reason she had come to consult me in the first place – I asked her whether there were any questions she would like to ask about any other areas of her life. She thought for a moment and then said that there was in fact one question which she had in mind. I cleared the mat of all the stones upon it, although I did not replace them in the tray with the others – and asked her to concentrate upon the question and, while doing so, to choose five further crystals or stones from the tray. Here is a diagram showing you the stones she selected:

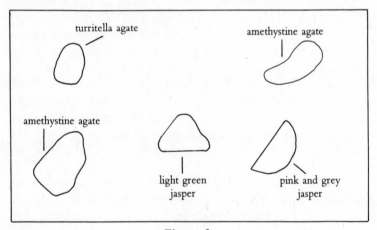

Figure 3

The first stone selected unhesitatingly from those which remained in the tray was the pink jasper lightly tinged with grey. Next came the turritella agate and the large amethystine agate, both of which Marianne placed on the opposite side of the mat to the pink jasper. After some reflection she chose another smaller piece of amethystine agate and then, almost at once, the lovely piece of light green jasper. This was placed fairly centrally on the mat, almost like a link between the two groups of stones already there.

Consider the stones in order of selection. The pink jasper refers, as we already know, to an older person who is of some significance in the questioner's life. Usually this turns out to be a parent, although sometimes it is another older person of whom the questioner is exceptionally fond. I told Marianne that I thought the question in her mind related to one of her parents and she agreed that it did actually concern her mother.

The turritella agate, the second stone to be chosen, indicated to me that the question also concerned Marianne's working life as this particular stone normally refers to some change in that area. I did not feel that Marianne was actually concerned about her abilities in the area of her career as there had been absolutely no indication of this in the original choice of crystals and stones. Glancing downwards to the next stone to be selected, I saw the largest of the amethystine agates in my collection. Now this particular stone, as you already know, is concerned with a move of home and – as Marianne had chosen the largest of my amethystine agates – I felt that the move was likely to take place soon.

Marianne confirmed what I had said. She was very happy in her career and was doing extremely well. In fact, young as she was, she was soon to be promoted to area manager within the same company. This was a great achievement and one which delighted the young woman. It would, however, require her to move as she would have to be based at the company's Head Office and this was in Oxford. This in itself did not worry her and she was quite looking forward to starting a new life with both a new home and a new position at the same time.

Obviously then the problem was not to do with Marianne herself but with her mother. Looking again at the selection of stones upon the mat, I saw another, smaller, piece of amethystine agate close to the pink jasper. I told Marianne that I thought her mother too was likely to move, although not quite as soon as Marianne herself – possibly anything up to a year later. Because there was a piece of light green jasper between the two groups of stones on the mat, I thought that the move seemed to be linked with Marianne's own and, taking into account the meaning of that light green jasper (which, as we have seen, is happiness), I felt that both moves, but in particular that of the older woman, would bring happiness in their wake.

Marianne looked relieved. Then she explained the problem to me. Although her mother at 62 was by no means an old woman, nonetheless she was growing older day by day. Marianne, being an only child, was a little concerned about how her mother would manage as time went on. At present they lived just a few streets apart and, although she did not see her mother all the time, Marianne did feel that she was able to keep an eye on her and that she was never too far away in case of emergency. The only worry that she had with regard to the promotion and the move to Oxford was that, should any problem concerning her mother arise, she would be too far away to be of any assistance. She had been trying to persuade her mother to move to Oxford too – not to live with her but at least to be nearby – but so far this attempt at persuasion had been to no avail. The older woman was an independent lady and did not want to feel, as she put it, that she would be a 'burden' to her daughter. However, she did not have any real friends in the area in which she now lived and Marianne had been trying to explain to her that, even if she moved to Oxford, she would not in fact be a burden. They would be two independent people leading their own lives but not so far away from each other that Marianne could not keep an eye on her mother and be on hand if she were needed.

I told Marianne that I did not think her mother would move at the same time as she did but that, within the following year, she would also come to Oxford and that the move would be a happy and successful one for her.

Some six months or so after her initial visit, Marianne telephoned and asked if she could come to see me for a further reading. When she arrived she told me that she had been living in Oxford for about two months, working at her new post in the Head Office of her company and thoroughly enjoying it. Her mother had finally realized that she would be more content living in the same town as her daughter and Marianne had in fact come to collect her to take her down for a few days of house-hunting. In the meantime she felt that she would like a further reading from me.

Once again she sat at my table and once again I asked her to select nine crystals or stones to place upon the mat.

As you will see from the diagram, the stones and crystals this time were placed upon the mat in one group – there were no

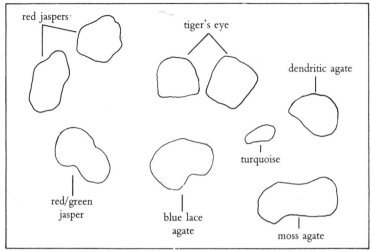

Figure 4

separate little groupings. This in itself is often a good sign, indicating a wholeness or oneness in the life of the questioner at that particular time.

The first stones to be chosen were the two red jaspers, followed very quickly by the two pieces of tiger's eye. Next came the blue lace agate and then the red and green jasper. There was then some hesitation before Marianne eventually chose, in quick succession, the turquoise, the dendritic agate and the moss agate.

Looking at the selection of crystals and stones, we can see that, once again, it is a reading which predominantly concerns Marianne's emotional life. But how good it was to watch her choose the two red jaspers first. These are the signs of love and depth of emotion. Now Marianne, as we know, had always been an emotional young woman but the fact that there were two of these glowing red jaspers convinced me that she had become more able to see love and affection around her than she had previously been. I felt that possibly there was now another man in her life and that, although naturally there would have been no total meta-morphosis in Marianne (as the continued presence of the red and green jasper showed), she was perhaps more able now to accept the possibility that someone for whom she cared would care for her in return. The red and green jasper portrayed a certain amount of emotional stress and fear but at least in this reading the positive stones outnumbered the negative ones.

Right in the centre of the mat, close to those red jaspers, were two fairly large pieces of tiger's eye. I felt from these that the man she cared for was a strong and somewhat independent character – quite possibly someone who had his own business. He also appeared to have a daughter as there was a delicate piece of blue lace agate close by.

Marianne was able to confirm this to some extent. Soon after she had arrived in Oxford she had become friendly with a young woman some five or six years her junior. This young woman had introduced Marianne to her father, a widower in his late forties who had his own design company in the city. Friendship and the beginnings of love had grown between the two of them but, because of past happenings in her life, Marianne felt unable to trust her judgement and had become very confused, being torn between her growing feelings for this man and her unhappy experiences of the past. She had come to me to see what I could glean from her choice of stones.

I was delighted to be able, because of the three remaining stones on the mat, to set Marianne's mind at rest. As you can see, they consist of a turquoise – contentment; a dendritic agate – sunshine and joy; and a moss agate – peace of mind. In other words, within this new relationship Marianne would find contentment, joy and peace of mind – at last.

3. Stuart

Stuart is a quietly-spoken man of about 35. He came to see me first approximately three years ago. Sitting at the table, he obviously took the whole process of selecting the nine crystals and stones from among those in the tray very seriously indeed. Each individual stone was picked up, turned over and over, and carefully considered before being either selected or rejected.

The first to be chosen were the two amethysts which he laid carefully – even lovingly – on the mat. Then came the agate geode and the rose quartz, followed by the long slender piece of aquamarine. A little more time for thinking, a few more stones turned over and studied and the turritella agate found its way to the mat, a little apart from the others already there. Then followed the white and amber agate and the agate with fossils embedded in it. Finally, with an expression almost of triumph, Stuart rummaged around among the contents of the tray and, from somewhere at the

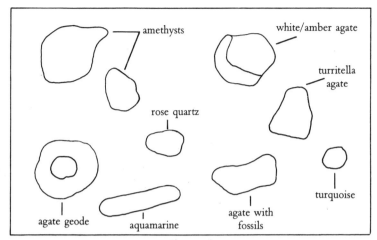

amethysts

white/amber agate

turritella agate

rose quartz

agate geode

aquamarine

agate with fossils

turquoise

Figure 5

bottom of the pile, produced a small turquoise.

Look at the diagram which shows the crystals and stones selected. What does this tell you about Stuart? The first two to be chosen – the two amethysts – are very strong indications of a person's spiritual side. The fact that there were two of them, coupled with the fact that they were the first to be chosen, made me think that to Stuart this was a very important part of his life. The presence of the agate geode, placed in such a way that its glittering interior could be seen, told me that Stuart was also a man of psychic ability and that he was already aware of this and perhaps had even been doing something about developing it. The lovely rose quartz – the healing stone – was also placed in that particular group which persuaded me that, as well as having psychic ability, Stuart could well have the ability to become a spiritual healer. Because of the positions of the crystals – with the rose quartz much nearer to the centre of the mat than the agate geode – I felt that it was this healing side which was of more importance to Stuart than any psychic ability that he might possess – although naturally the two quite often go hand in hand.

I explained my feelings to Stuart and he agreed that he was aware of a certain degree of psychic ability developing within him and, although he had spent some time trying to encourage this development still further, it was the idea of becoming a healer which really appealed to him.

I looked again at the rose quartz and noted the presence of the aquamarine immediately below it. The aquamarine is the crystal of common sense, of the intellect, of knowledge. In what way did this relate to Stuart's healing and his desire to pursue it still further? I felt that, although Stuart would be able to become quite adept at traditional spiritual healing, at the laying of hands either on the physical body or on the aura, he would work best at something which linked his natural healing ability and his very real commonsense approach to life. He seemed to need a practical base to his healing and I suggested that either becoming a therapist or some sort of counsellor would successfully combine both sides of his nature and that the healing of minds and emotions is just as important as the healing of bodies.

Stuart responded immediately to this idea. It was something he had not really considered until that moment. He had thought that he would continue throughout his life working at his office job during the day and developing and using his healing talent during his spare time. The fact that it might actually be possible to spend his working life doing what he most wanted to do – making people feel better – was like the opening of a new window to him – and the view was exciting.

As if bearing out my thoughts, the piece of turritella agate sat there on the mat, telling me that there would indeed be a change of occupation for Stuart. However, I did not think that it would be immediate – nor would I ever advise anyone to leave their employment and take a chance without going into matters very carefully indeed. One of the main reasons for the delay – apart from the necessity for careful consideration – seemed to be indicated by the presence of the white and amber agate placed immediately above the turritella agate. This stone represents books, reading and writing and I felt that perhaps Stuart would be drawn to taking a course in some kind of therapy to enable him to do the type of work which would bring him real satisfaction. Stuart confirmed that this would be likely as, if indeed he did decide to become either a counsellor or a therapist, he would do it properly and study in order to become proficient in whatever he decided to undertake. He asked me whether I really felt that there would be an opportunity for him to do this sort of work for a living and I said that it would be more than possible. This fact was born out by the presence of the agate with fossils – the money stone – linking the change of job with the healing and the practical side of his nature.

As if in final confirmation of what I had so far felt, the pretty little turquoise of contentment was there among the other crystals and stones, indicating to me that Stuart would be far happier with his new way of life than he had ever thought possible.

Like a child with a new toy to play with, Stuart kept repeating over and over that the idea seemed wonderful to him. He could not understand how it was that he had never before thought of combining both sides of his life to give him both a way of earning his living and also complete personal satisfaction.

Since we seemed to have covered that topic fully, I asked Stuart what other aspect of his life he would like me to discuss or whether, indeed, he had any specific questions he would like to ask. He told me that he did in fact have another area on which he would like guidance and, as usual, I asked him to concentrate upon that particular situation and to choose another five crystals or stones from those remaining in the tray. Those he chose are illustrated in the following diagram:

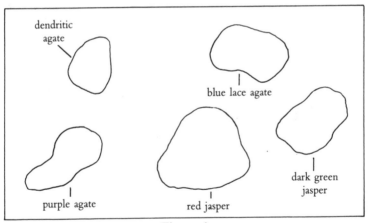

Figure 6

The first two stones to be chosen by Stuart as he concentrated upon his question were the blue lace agate and the dark green jasper. I felt therefore that there was some concern or anxiety in his mind to do with a young girl, possibly a daughter. The presence of the large red jasper just beside the first two stones also indicated a strength of feeling for that person. Stuart agreed that, yes, he did have a daughter about whom he cared very deeply and that, as he and his wife had divorced some two years earlier, he did not see his little girl as often as he would have liked. His parting with his former wife had been somewhat stormy and he hoped that nothing had happened to turn his daughter against him. What he really wanted to know was whether there would be an opportunity in the comparatively near future for him to spend some time with his child – he was unable to see her on a regular basis as they lived 300 miles apart.

If you look again at the diagram, you will see that Stuart had picked the golden yellow dendritic agate and placed it right in the centre of the mat. As you know, if this particular stone is selected in answer to a question, then the answer will always be the one desired by the questioner. In this case, I felt that it would certainly be possible for Stuart to spend more time with his daughter in the near future and, taking note of the presence of the purple agate – the stone which represents water in some form –'I thought that it would be possible that Stuart and his little girl might have a holiday together – possibly by the sea.

Stuart looked a little uncertain. Certainly a holiday with his daughter was something he would have liked very much indeed but he did not think that his ex-wife would ever agree to such a thing. However, as he put it, he was prepared to 'wait and see'.

Before he left, Stuart asked me whether he could ask one further question. Once again he chose five crystals or stones from the tray and placed them on the mat.

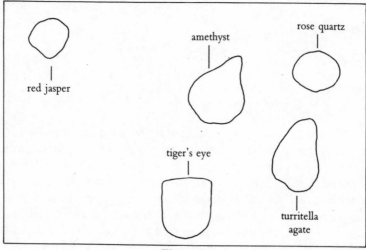

Figure 7

Stuart chose the first four stones almost together and placed them on the right-hand side of the mat. Then, after thinking for some time and hunting around in the tray – as if searching for something which did not exist – he came up with a small red jasper and set it down, all alone, almost in the very corner of the mat.

The first four to be selected were easy to understand. Once again we see the amethyst and the rose quartz – the crystals of spirituality and of healing. Once again we see a turritella agate which signifies a change of work. This time we also see a piece of tiger's eye showing us that Stuart was quite likely to end up by working for himself in his chosen 'healing' career.

All that was easy to understand. However, all alone in one corner of the mat – so near the corner as to be almost off the mat altogether – was that small red jasper. It was the smallest of the jaspers in my collection and it was a clear, perfect red. The red jasper being the stone of love and deep emotions, I asked Stuart whether there was a new love in his life. He replied that there was not – and that he did not feel that he was interested in forming any deep attachment for the time being. It seemed to me, because of the presence of that clear red jasper, that there would indeed be a new romance in Stuart's life in the not-too-distant future and that this time it would be a relationship far less troubled by complications than his marriage had been. As he had picked such a small jasper, however, and as he had placed it almost 'out of the picture', I felt that the other aspects of his life were far more important to him at that time and that the next year or so would be spent in consolidating the growing ideas and abilities which were already developing within him.

Some time later Stuart telephoned me to tell me how he was getting on. He informed me that he had given up his office job and was undergoing full-time training in psychotherapy, intending to work as a therapist and counsellor when the course was completed. It was not easy, as he told me, becoming a student again after so long, but nonetheless he was really happy to be doing what he felt was the right thing for him and he was looking forward to the time when he would be able to practise professionally. He still had no indication of any romance in his life but felt that, in any event, he would not want it at that time. As to whether it would knock at his door at some later date, naturally he could not yet know. Oh, and by the way, his ex-wife had suddenly and unexpectedly agreed to his little girl coming to spend a fortnight of her school holidays with him, and Stuart had taken her to Cornwall for a week of that time, much to the delight of both father and daughter.

4. Michael and Daphne

They came to see me together. Michael was an earnest-looking young man in his early thirties and Daphne was a pale, gentle girl with incredibly sad eyes. He did all the talking, asking whether it would be possible for me to do a reading for the two of them together. He said that they had been married for seven years, had a three-year-old son and their own home – but lately things had not been too good between them and could I help?

I explained to them that I never give readings for two people together, or even for one if the other is in the room. There are two reasons for this: the first is that, on a spiritual level, it is quite possible to pick up vibrations from one when talking to the other – particularly if the two people are closely linked. The other reason is that I feel that it inhibits me in what I say, particularly if I think that something I say is likely to be hurtful to the other person. It also inhibits the questioner in what he or she feels free to say. If I were to give a reading to a husband who was being unfaithful to his wife, for example, and his wife was sitting beside him, I would feel very hesitant about hurting her feelings by saying what I saw – and the husband would, presumably, feel equally awkward about the truth coming out in the course of his reading.

I explained my feelings to Michael and Daphne and said that the only thing I felt I could do for them was to give each of them a separate reading, after which, if they wished, they could discuss whatever points had arisen. Hopefully, that discussion might point to a solution of their joint problems. They agreed to this idea and Daphne went off to sit in another room while Michael remained with me to have his reading.

The first stone Michael selected – and he did so with no hesitation whatsoever – was the dark green jasper. He placed this firmly in the upper right-hand section of the mat. The next five stones were also chosen fairly rapidly and these were placed in turn in a circle around that dark green jasper. Then there was a pause. After some moments Michael chose the red jasper and the agate quartz and put them close together on the left side of the

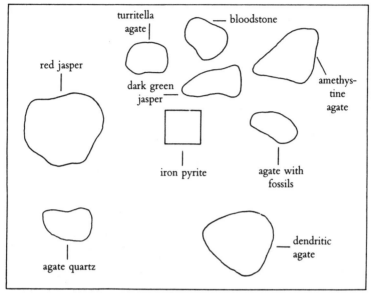

Figure 8

mat. Then there was a much longer pause. Various stones were handled somewhat diffidently and rejected with little ceremony. Finally Michael reached in among the remaining crystals and stones and came up with the golden dendritic agate. He turned this over and over in his hand, went to replace it among the others in the tray and then, at the last moment, changed his mind and placed it, all alone, in the bottom right-hand corner of the mat.

There is great significance in the fact that the first stone to be chosen was the dark green jasper, and also that it was chosen so unhesitatingly. That particular stone indicates anxiety or worry on the part of the questioner and I felt that Michael was definitely feeling under quite considerable pressure. I looked at the stones immediately surrounding that dark green jasper to see what light they could throw on the situation. There was a turritella agate, indicating a possible change of job, an amethystine agate showing a possible move of home and an agate with fossils which would seem to show that there was a likelihood of more money. On the surface they all appeared to be quite positive moves and yet, nestling there right in the centre of that little group of stones was that anxious dark green jasper.

Also part of the same group was the bloodstone. As you know, this can refer to physical aches and pains or even those which result from outside pressures and stress rather than from a physical cause. I felt, in this particular instance, that stress and tension was the cause and that any physical symptoms Michael might be experiencing could well be a direct result of that tension.

The last member of that cluster of stones was the iron pyrite – the stone that is often an indication that it is time to stop and take heed.

I felt that many of the changes indicated by that particular group of stones were likely, but that the whole thing seemed to be getting too much for Michael and that he was allowing himself to worry about all of them.

When I put this to Michael he agreed with me with something akin to relief. He told me that he was so worried and so unsure of which way to turn that he was not sleeping at night and he seemed to have an almost permanent headache.

Michael had worked for some years for his present company and had risen slowly and steadily through the ranks until he held quite a good position. Now an opportunity had arisen for a quite considerable improvement, both in status and salary, but it would mean moving to another part of the country. Michael had so many worries, he told me, that he just did not know which to mention first. First of all he was frightened that he would be unable to do the job well if and when he accepted the offer. Secondly, he was unsure about how to tell Daphne about the possibility of a move as he did not think she would want to leave the home they had built up over the years of their married life. In addition, he told me, Daphne was extremely attached to her mother who lived nearby and, as the move would be one of several hundred miles, naturally mother and daughter would see less of each other. Another concern was his own health. Logic told him that it was the worry itself which was causing the insomnia and the pressure he was feeling – but suppose it was not. He would be taking his wife and young son to a place hundreds of miles away where they knew nobody; he would be taking on a job which he did not even know if he could handle; suppose, on top of all that, his own health were to fail so that he was not able to cope with the job at all – what would happen then?

I looked again at the stones on the mat and there, immediately below the group of 'anxieties' was the piece of dendritic agate.

This is always a positive stone and one which denotes achievement and success. I told Michael that I had no worries whatsoever about his ability to cope with the responsibilities of his new job. To set his own mind at rest, I suggested that he went for a complete medical check-up, but I assured him that there was nothing that I could see in the reading to indicate poor physical health, except for the extreme tension and anxiety that seemed to surround him.

I went on to consider the last two stones on the mat – the ones that were placed apart from all the others on the left-hand side. There was a lovely clear, red jasper, indicating warmth of emotion and love, and an agate quartz, denoting a young boy – presumably his son. I told Michael that I thought there was no doubt as to the depth of feeling for his wife and child and that, although he was concerned about uprooting them, this was the one area of his life where he ought to be feeling secure.

At this a look of real sadness came into Michael's eyes. All he wanted, he told me, was to be with Daphne and their son and to be happy with them. And yet he felt he was losing them. Ever since they had met at college, he and Daphne had always been able to talk and had always found it easy to show their warm feelings for each other. But, just lately, Daphne seemed to have withdrawn into herself and they were not communicating as well as they had done previously. Even their love-life seemed to be different; there were often times now when Daphne appeared to be making excuses to avoid physical contact with him.

I asked Michael whether he had told Daphne about the possibility of the new position and the move. He said that he had not; he had been waiting for the right moment and it had never seemed to come. And the longer it went on, the more difficult it became to find that right moment.

I reiterated that I did not feel he should worry about his ability to cope with the new job or the move and I suggested that he ask the stones a direct question about whatever was causing him most concern. He seemed to have great difficulty in formulating the question and eventually, when he did, he spoke almost in a whisper. 'What about my marriage?', he said, 'What about my wife and my son?'

I told Michael to ask that question once more and then to choose just three stones from those in the tray. He thought for a moment or two and then picked up three stones and placed them in a straight line on the mat.

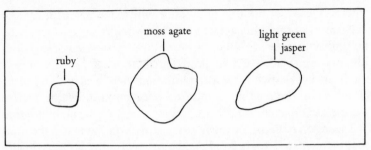

Figure 9

The first stone was the ruby. This indicated to me that Michael was being too hard on himself and expecting to be too perfect. I suggested that perhaps he would find things much easier to cope with if he and Daphne could just talk them over together.

Beside the ruby was the moss agate. The moss agate is the sign of peace of mind. This was followed by the light green jasper indicating happiness in a given situation. Bearing in mind Michael's question, I told him that I did not think he had anything to worry about so far as his marriage was concerned – but I did think it important that he talk to Daphne as soon as possible, before the rift between them became any greater.

Michael seemed really relieved. He told me that he had no further questions he wanted to ask and he was now very anxious for Daphne to have her reading as soon as possible. He almost rushed from the room and, moments later, Daphne came quietly in and sat, eyes downcast, at the table.

Slowly, and with trembling fingers, Daphne selected her nine stones from those in the tray. First to emerge was the large red, yellow and green jasper. Beside this was placed the piece of coal-black tektite. Then came the agate quartz.

Next Daphne chose the large red jasper, setting this down at the far side of the mat. Quickly in succession came the citrine quartz and the iron pyrite, but it took a little longer for her to select the dark green jasper and place it with the others. After making these choices, Daphne seemed to hesitate, as though she could not find any other stones she liked. Eventually she took the amethystine agate and the turquoise and put them so close to the corner of the mat that they were practically lying on the table itself.

As you have already learned, that large jasper with its streaks of red, green and yellow, is a indication of emotional vulnerability. It

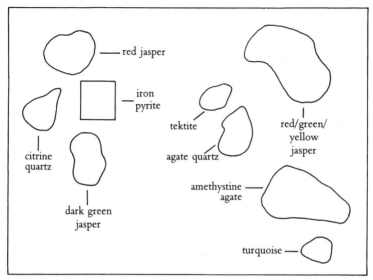

red jasper

iron
pyrite

tektite

agate quartz

red/green/
yellow
jasper

citrine
quartz

amethystine
agate

dark green
jasper

turquoise

Figure 10

is usually selected by someone who has been quite badly hurt on an emotional level and who is, perhaps, anxious that the same thing should not occur again. Beside that stone lay the piece of tektite, almost always a sign of depression in the questioner – whether past, or present or future. In this case, because it was one of the first stones chosen, I felt that it had more to do with Daphne's past than with her future. In particular, when I saw the agate quartz, which would have referred to her young son, close by, I asked her whether perhaps his birth had caused her to feel some measure of depression. Daphne said that she had, in fact, suffered from post-natal depression after Daniel's birth but that both Michael and her mother had been extremely helpful to her and the condition had passed. She was left with an underlying fear, however, that she was not as good a mother as she should be to Daniel and that she had somehow done him some harm during those first few months when she felt so depressed that she had been unable to cope. I reassured her by telling her that the indications were that the depression and anxiety she had suffered appeared to be in the past rather than in the present or the future and that I was quite sure her love for her young son was very real and that would make her a good a mother as anyone can be.

I then turned to look at the next little group of stones – those on the left. Once again, just as her husband had done, Daphne had chosen the dark green jasper of anxiety and worry. Grouped around this stone were the citrine quartz, indicating a change of direction in some respect, and the iron pyrite of misplaced trust. Included in this group, however, was the large red jasper, which is indicative of love and deeply-felt emotion. I told her that I thought there was some anxiety on her part concerning her love-life and a fear that there might be a change in deeper feelings. I did not think that there was actually going to be a change in those feelings, but mainly because of that ominous dark green jasper, I did believe that her anxiety was very real.

When I told her this she burst into tears. It was true, she told me. She knew that Michael was keeping something from her, but she did not know what it was. Always ready to blame herself, she thought that perhaps Michael did not love her any more and that he had found someone else. 'I wouldn't blame him if he had', she told me. 'I never knew what he saw in me anyway.' Because of her feeling that Michael was staying with her out of duty to her and their small son, she found that she could not respond to him in the way that she used to and, naturally, this had only served to aggravate the problem.

I told Daphne that I felt her fears were unjustified and that her reading did not indicate any loss of feeling on Michael's part – only her fear that this was happening. Due to her own lack of confidence, brought about in great measure by her bout of post-natal depression, she had immediately jumped to the conclusion that Michael must find her unlovable and, because she was sensitive enough to realize that he was actually hiding something from her, she thought that he had, in fact, found someone else to love.

Turning to consider the last two stones on the mat, I explained to Daphne that the amethystine agate was normally present when there was to be a move of home and that the little turquoise nestling beside it showed that, if that move did take place, it would be one which would bring her great tranquillity and peace of mind.

Daphne looked puzzled. She did not see why they should need to move from their present home. But she told me that she was prepared to wait and see what happened. I asked her how she would feel about a move and she replied that she was not

particularly bothered one way or the other – all that mattered to
her was her happiness with Michael and Daniel.

I asked Daphne whether she had any specific questions which
she felt she would like to ask. She had only one. If they were
indeed going to move, she presumed it would be quite a long
distance away as, if they were staying in the area, there would be
no need to find another house. In that case, what would happen to
her mother? Her mother had been a great help to her when she had
been suffering from the post-natal depression and they saw each
other quite frequently. As she was an only child, Daphne,
naturally, was concerned about how her mother would cope.

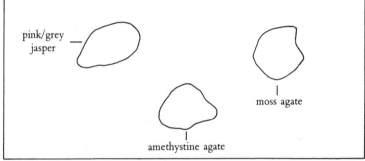

pink/grey
jasper

moss agate

amethystine agate

Figure 11

I asked Daphne to select three further stones from among those
in the tray. She chose the pink and grey jasper, a slightly smaller
amethystine agate than the one that had appeared in her own
reading, and a green and white moss agate.

The pink and grey jasper, as you know, refers to an older person
– usually a woman. The amethystine agate indicates a move of
home and the moss agate peace of mind. Because the amethystine
agate chosen in answer to this particular question was smaller than
the one selected by Daphne herself, I felt that, although it seemed
evident that her mother would also move home, it would not be at
the same time as her own move but somewhat later. I also felt that
this move would give peace of mind to them both.

I then asked Michael to come into the room with Daphne and I
explained to them that I never revealed the contents of one
person's reading to anyone else – even when the other person is
the husband or wife of the questioner. I told them, however, that I
thought that a great many of their problems had come about

because of lack of communication between the two of them and that, because of this failure to speak to each other about those topics which really mattered, many misunderstandings had arisen. I suggested that they went home, told each other what had been in their own readings and discussed whatever arose with complete honesty. I knew, because of the love for each other which had shown itself so clearly in the course of both readings, that they would not be disappointed in the outcome.

I never heard from Michael again but, some little time later, Daphne came to see me to tell me what had taken place. Apparently she and her husband had had a very emotional discussion when each had told the other of their secret fears. Each of them had been astonished at what the other had said. They had both been so wrapped up in their own anxious thoughts that the simple truth had not been apparent to either of them. They had discussed Michael's prospective new move within his job and had decided jointly that the prospects seemed good and that it was well worth taking advantage of the opportunity. Plans were made for a move of home, their own home had already been sold and they hoped to leave in about four weeks' time. The whole matter had been discussed also with Daphne's mother and it had been decided that, once the young couple had settled into their new home, she would make plans to move too. Daphne was her only child and Daniel her only grandchild so she felt that she had nothing to keep her in her present home. Apparently, she intended to try and find a bungalow not too far away from her daughter and, although Daphne was now quite able to cope with her son, it gave an added boost to her confidence to think that her mother would soon be living near to her.

Michael's fears about his health were fast disappearing. The headaches had vanished completely and he was sleeping better. He would always be a worrier, as would Daphne, but at least they had agreed to try and discuss their worries where possible so that unfounded fears did not manifest themselves again in the future. Daphne might never, without help, be a fully confident person, but her worst fears had turned out to be quite unfounded and the world she most cherished – that of husband, son and mother – was once again secure.

So, once again, you can see how using the stones and crystals can enable you to help others – not by telling them what to do, but by using a combination of the meanings of the stones themselves and whatever spiritual help *you* are receiving, to point them in the right direction so that they can, in fact, help themselves.

One of the problems encountered by so many people these days is how to make the correct choice of job or career. At one time it would have been safe to say that this was a problem primarily of the young, but in this, the age of redundancy, employment difficulties and working wives and mothers, it is, in fact, a problem facing those of all ages and types. No longer does a young man leave school and embark on a form of employment that will occupy him until he reaches the age of retirement. It is common nowadays to find many people changing career mid-stream – not that that is altogether a bad thing. How much better to find, as one changes within oneself, that one is also able to change the way in which one works.

In this area too the crystals and stones can prove extremely helpful. Over the past year or two, I have dealt with many cases of people coming to consult me to ask for help in making decisions about the future direction of their working life. Naturally, it is not my task – nor would it be yours – to tell anyone precisely how to run their working life and what path to follow. What I do find that the stones enable me to do is to give very strong and definite indications of the particular abilities and the potential of the questioner, as well as in which areas he or she would be happiest to work. It must be emphasized, however, that this is offered as a form of guidance for the questioner rather than an attempt to make up the person's mind for him or her.

People of all ages can be helped in this way – from the very young to those approaching retirement. I do not work with children under the age of about twelve or thirteen as I feel that they are so suggestible and changeable that it would be wrong to place too much emphasis on any one aspect of their lives. It is important for children to keep open as many options and possibilities as they can. When they reach the age of twelve or thirteen, however, young people are compelled to begin to make choices. Schools insist that they select the subjects on which they wish to concentrate for the remainder of their school lives. It is at this point that the crystals and stones can prove helpful in showing the potential of the young person concerned.

The next age-group to consider is that of young people who are about to leave school without going on to further education. Often those in this group feel that they are the neglected ones, the ones who are somehow left out of the system and, by using the crystals and stones to help them, not only can you give them an indication of the direction in which they would be happiest to head, but it is possible to give them some sort of hope for the future.

In this era of working women, there are many who find themselves eager to take up a working life again once their children are old enough to be in full-time education or to be left with someone competent to look after them. These women will have matured considerably since leaving work to start their families and, unless the career they were following prior to having children was particularly satisfying, they will be looking for a new direction. Because they have been out of the working world for several years, however, many women feel that they do not have the confidence to make choices and are anxiously looking for help. I think that this is perhaps the type of person who has been to consult me most frequently in search of some assistance with planning their working future.

'Redundancy' is a terrible and all-too-common word these days. Although those who are made redundant may have been excellent at their jobs, and although the loss of employment may not have been in any way their fault (perhaps a company has gone into liquidation), nonetheless it has never been easy (and is even less so at this particular time) for a man or woman of middle age to find another job, however proficient he or she may be in his or her own particular sphere. Many of these people have to change direction completely – some of them have become so disillusioned with the work they were doing that they very much *want* to change direction – and, because circumstances will have eroded their natural confidence, this type of person also is in need of some help and guidance as to which direction to take.

The other category of person who can be helped particularly by consulting the crystals and stones is the man or woman who has reached an age where he or she is forced to retire from the employment they have been involved in – sometimes for many years. Sixty or sixty-five is no great age these days and people just do not want to be idle for the rest of their days – they, as much as anyone else, need a sense of purpose and something more to do with their time than indulge in hobbies, which may be pleasant enough but are not sufficient to fulfill their needs.

Each and every type of individual so far mentioned is quite capable of being helped considerably by you with the aid of your crystals and stones. People who fall into each of the categories mentioned have been to consult me in the last year or so for just this sort of help. And in each case, without my actually telling anyone precisely what they should do for, as I have said, I do not consider this ever to be my task, each has gone away to find some sort of fulfilment in the direction they have been helped to choose themselves.

So how does it work? How do I – and how will you – use the lovely crystals and stones to help those who come to consult us? The method is quite different to that used for guidance as to the future generally.

The first thing I ask the questioner to do is to sit with the stones and sort them into three piles – the ones he or she likes particularly, the ones he or she does not like at all and, finally, those to which he or she is indifferent or about which he or she does not feel strongly enough to either like or dislike.

If one is dealing with someone, of whatever age, where their self-confidence has been totally sapped, it is not unusual to find that all the crystals and stones end up in either the 'dislike' or the 'indifferent' piles. If this occurs, I usually spend a little time talking to the questioner and pointing out to him that he is being less than honest and that I do not believe that there is not one crystal or stone that he likes. I then suggest that the questioner selects just one stone, the one that he likes the best, and places it to one side. Once the questioner has been persuaded – however gently – into action, he will normally continue sorting the stones in the way desired and will end up with three piles of stones as requested in the first instance.

So now you have your three groups of crystals and stones in front of you. Look first at the ones that the questioner has said that he actively dislikes. Those are the stones that will give an indication of areas that he should avoid with regard to work unless compelled by circumstances to encompass them in what he does. It does not mean that any harm would come to him if the work were to involve any or all of these things, merely that he would not be likely to feel as content or fulfilled in his work if they were to play too great a part.

Now look at the second group, the one containing the crystals and stones selected by the questioner as the ones he actually likes – those which are his favourites. Here you will find very definite indications of the areas where the questioner will be happiest, where he is likely to find the greatest career satisfaction. That does not mean, naturally, that he will ever be able to find a single job that is going to incorporate all the desired elements, but at least he knows where to start looking.

What about the remaining group? Here you have a selection of crystals and stones about which the questioner feels nothing in particular. What is their significance? Among them you will find those elements of a possible job or career that would not necessarily be those which the questioner would choose but, equally would not cause him any great displeasure should they become part of his working life.

Below are actual case histories of clients (their names, naturally, have been changed) with whom I have worked in the recent past. By showing you, in each case, which crystals and stones the person concerned placed in which pile, and by telling you the conclusions that were reached as a result of that selection, I hope that you will be able to see the value of this form of consultation and the effect it had on the lives of three different people, each of them anxious to set out on a new path and somewhat unsure of which signpost to follow.

5. Gemma

A small, slim thirteen-year-old, with huge hazel eyes, Gemma was brought to see me by her parents. In no instance would I be prepared to do any sort of reading or any consultation for someone of this tender age unless the parents not only knew about it but also accompanied her.

The reason for the visit was that Gemma, at thirteen, was in the position of having to make deliberate selections at school as to the subjects she wished to study and, while the child herself knew in which direction she would like her career to go, the parents were unsure that she was choosing wisely but did not wish to force their daughter to change her mind unless there seemed to be good reason for doing so. I explained that I would not be telling any of them what they should do, but only giving an indication of what seemed to be Gemma's particular talents and abilities.

Having explained to Gemma what I wanted her to do with her parents present, I asked her parents to leave the room while she made her selection from my tray of crystals and stones, so that she could do so without feeling that she was being watched. That having been accomplished, I asked her parents to return so that I could talk to all of them together about the meaning of the various choices indicated by the stones Gemma had picked. Gemma's choices were:

1. Those she liked:
Rutilated quartz (artistic ability)
Tiger's eye (independence)
Botswana agate (pleasure, enthusiasm)
Red jasper (emotions, joy, love)
Labradorite (overseas travel)
Aquamarine (common sense)
Dendritic agate (success, achievement)
Quartz crystal (energy)

2. Those she disliked:
Red/green/yellow jasper (anxiety)
Petrified wood (legal matters)
Iron pyrite (folly, mistrust)
Tektite (despair)
Bloodstone (health conditions)
Turritella agate (change of work)
Pink and grey jasper (concerning older people)
Dark green jasper (worry)

The remainder of the stones fell into the middle category – neither particularly liked nor disliked.

I looked first of all at the group of stones indicating what Gemma liked, had a talent for and was happiest with. The first stone to be chosen had been the rutilated quartz, showing artistic or creative ability. Combining this with the quartz crystal, denoting energy, and the dendritic agate of success, I felt that she would be willing to put all her zeal and energy into a career that made the most of her artistic talent. The tiger's eye showed an independent nature and the labradorite that there were possibilities of a career where travel overseas might be likely. I was pleased to see the aquamarine there in the pile of Gemma's favourite stones, as this showed that she had a sensible and a logical as well as an artisic side and that her head was not just full of a young girl's dreams of pursuing an artistic career. It also seemed to be important to Gemma that she followed the career that would make her happy rather than the one that would necessarily bring her the most money. The agate with fossils – the little money stone – was not, however, among the stones that Gemma actively disliked; this told me that, although money was not of prime importance, she was not so dreamy that she disregarded it altogether. The remaining stone was the amethystine agate, which normally indicates a move of home. As she was still only thirteen, I asked Gemma's parents whether there was perhaps some possibility of her going away from home to study. They agreed that this was, in fact, so.

Next, I turned my attention to the stones that Gemma did not like at all. Among them I saw the piece of petrified wood, which is to with law, legal matters and so on. I felt that any career in this, or any similar, direction would be the last thing that Gemma would want. Also there were the stones to do with old people and ill-health and, although Gemma was quite a caring and compassionate young girl, I felt that her very sensitivity would make it difficult for her to work in any caring capacity where she would be likely to come into day-to-day contact with sickness or depressive problems.

Gemma's parents then told me that their daughter was extremely anxious to pursue a theatrical career, but that they were deeply concerned – firstly because it is such a precarious profession and, secondly, because although Gemma had been winning medals, certificates and trophies for her singing, dancing and acting talents since the age of six, they did not want to be 'pushy' parents or to lull themselves into a false sense of optimism when their daughter's talent might not justify it.

I pointed out to them that the crystals and stones indicated that Gemma's talent was, in fact, real and that she appeared to be sensible enough and dedicated enough to work hard in order to achieve her chosen aims. I felt that her career would indeed give her great joy and would lead to a certain amount of overseas travel.

The move of *home* indicated actually turned out to be a move of *school*. Gemma's parents told me that she had been offered a place at a well-known theatrical boarding-school, which would mean her living away from home during termtime. The school was one that concentrated on the academic side of life as well as the artistic, so Gemma's education would not suffer in that direction – a very necessary thing to take into consideration considering the precariousness of the theatrical world. The presence of the aquamarine among Gemma's chosen stones led me to the belief that she was indeed sensible enough to see the logic of taking academic examinations and working hard in that respect too and that she would be only too ready to do so if it meant that she would have the opportunity to pursue the career on which she had set her heart.

Gemma, naturally, was delighted that the crystals and stones had borne out what she wanted so much for herself and her parents felt comforted and reassured that they were in fact doing the best thing for their daughter.

When I next heard from the family, about a year later, Gemma was doing extremely well at her new school and was studying for five academic O levels in addition to concentrating on training for her theatrical career. At the same time Gemma sent me some tickets for a professional pantomime in which she had been given a small part.

6. Christopher

Christopher had worked continuously for the same commercial organization from the time he left college. About ten months before he came to see me, at the age of forty-four, he had been told that the firm was to go into liquidation and that, although he would receive a considerable amount of redundancy pay, he would be without a job. To Christopher, with a wife, three children and a mortgage, this, naturally, had come as a terrible blow. At first he had thought that, because of his educational background, he would not have too much difficulty in finding another position. But, as the months had gone by, he had become more depressed and felt more hopeless about his prospects.

The fact that he was not at all sure that I would be able to help him in any way showed very clearly on his face as he came into the room. He sat heavily in the chair opposite me and listened half-heartedly as I explained what he had to do.

When he had finished sorting out the crystals and stones into their separate piles, I looked and saw that there were only two groups of stones on the mat. Christopher explained that there were a few he disliked but most of them had been placed in the 'don't know' group. This was obviously a clear indication of the hopelessness that Christopher was feeling but it was of no use either to me or to him when it came to trying to help him sort out something for his future.

I told Christopher that I just did not believe that there was nothing in life that he would enjoy, given the opportunity to do so, and I suggested that I went and made each of us a cup of coffee while he looked through the stones again and put them into the *three* groups I had asked for. When I returned I was relieved to find he had actually done what I had asked.

1. Stones he liked:
Petrified wood (legal, academic subjects)
Citrine quartz (new direction)
White and amber agate (books)
Tiger's eye (independence)
Aquamarine (logic, intellect)
Agate with fossils (money)
Ruby (self-criticism, perfectionism)
Quartz crystal (energy)

2. Those he did not like:
Amethystine agate (move of home)
Turritella agate (change of job)
Tektite (anxiety, despair)
Iron pyrite (misplaced trust)
Labradorite (overseas travel)

Looking first at the stones telling me what Christopher was in fact likely to enjoy and to do well at, the first thing to spring to my notice was the tiger's eye, indicating a need for independence and to be his own person. That is quite a logical desire on the part of a man who had been employed by a company and who had (in his own words) been 'thrown away' because the *company* had failed rather than because of any failure on his part. He agreed that he was quite determined that this would never happen to him again.

The presence of the agate with fossils demonstrated a very real need for money and for financial security. Once again this was quite understandable. Christopher had quite substantial home and family commitments, as have most men by the time they reach his age, and one of the hardest things for him to bear over the previous months had been the knowledge that, although his redundancy payment had been considerable, it could not last for ever and he did not know how he would then be able to cope with his responsibilities.

The citrine quartz showed that it seemed to be necessary for Christopher to go in a new direction as far as his career was concerned – away from being the rising executive employed by a vast company and perhaps into something that was more personal. This was borne out by looking at the stones Christopher actually disliked. There you will see the labradorite indicating travel, and the amethystine agate meaning a change of home. Christopher agreed that he had had his fill of travelling around on business and that he felt a great desire to settle in one place and pursue a less high-powered career.

The presence of the petrified wood among the stones that Christopher favoured showed a particular interest in either legal or academic matters. This was emphasized by the piece of white and amber agate that is specifically concerned with books or writing. The aquamarine close by indicated that Christopher would be happier making use of his ability to think clearly and logically as part of his work. All these things made great sense to Christopher who told me that his grandfather had been a headmaster, his father a University lecturer and that he himself had always had a liking for all things academic and, particularly when he was younger, for literature and history.

The fact that there was a piece of quartz crystal in the pile of 'likes' proved to me that Christopher would use all his energies to make a success of whatever he did – if only he could discover what that something should be! The last stone in the group was a small ruby, which can be an indication of perfectionism in the questioner or, taken to its extreme, of him being far too hard on himself. I felt that this might be a slight warning to Christopher not to feel that something was beyond him if it was what he really wanted to do.

Turning now to the rest of the stones for which Christopher felt an actual dislike, as well as the labradorite and the amethystine agate already mentioned, there is a turritella agate indicating change of employment, the iron pyrite of deception or let-down and a piece of tektite, which means despair. These combined to tell me that this would be the wrong time for Christopher to become part of a large company again as he would never have faith that the same thing could not happen all over again and that he would not have to face the disappointment and despair of being out of work when he had done his very best for his employers. It also served to reinforce the belief that, if at all possible, Christopher should try and find some way of working for himself.

I asked Christopher whether there was sufficient of the redundancy money left to enable him to set himself up in some way and whether he had thought of doing so. He said that there was indeed sufficient finance to set himself up in a small business and that he had considered it, but his confidence seemed to have been so shattered that he thought he might be making an unwise decision. Besides, he did not know what he would be capable of doing, and he certainly did not want to go back to his previous career with all its pressures and uncertainties.

When Christopher left me at the end of the consultation, he seemed to think that little had been achieved but he promised to go away and think over all that had been discussed. Just two short weeks later he telephoned me and said that he had been given the opportunity to buy a small bookshop from the present owner who was retiring. He felt that this was something he would really like to do but he wanted reassurance that it fitted in with what I had seen in stones. I told him that I thought it would fit in very well and wished him luck with his project.

Some time later Christopher came to see me again to introduce a friend who wanted a reading. While he was with me he told me that, although he was by no means on the way to becoming a millionaire, the bookshop was, in fact, making sufficient money for him and his family to live on and that he was more content with his way of life than he had been for years.

7. Edith

Edith was a lovely lady of sixty-eight. She looked rather like a picture-book granny with soft white hair and twinkling blue eyes. She came into my room, sat at my table and promptly told me that she was being silly! When I asked what she meant, she said, 'I have nothing to worry about. I am quite comfortable financially. I have close contact with all my family, although they have all grown up and left home now – but I need something more'.

It appeared that Edith had, in her younger days, been a nursing sister. She had married a man who had adored her, had brought up three children and had good relations with all of them, as well as with her vast number of friends and acquaintances. Her husband had died some four years earlier, leaving her well provided for and with a lovely home. But she felt, in her words, 'useless'. She was not the type to spend her days pottering in the garden and attending coffee mornings. She was not particularly concerned about money, but she felt that she needed to be occupied in some fulfilling way during the day.

Edith thought that the whole idea of helping herself through the crystals and stones was great fun and she entered into it wholeheartedly.

1. Those she liked:
Amethyst (spiritual)
Rose quartz (healing)
Aquamarine (clear thought)
Moss agate (peace of mind)
Turquoise (contentment)
Light green jasper (happiness)

2. Those she disliked:
This was much more difficult – as Edith said, 'But they're all so pretty'. On being asked which of the stones she liked least, she was able to select only four.

Tiger's eye (independence)
Petrified wood (legal or academic matters)
Agate with fossils (money)
White and amber agate (books)

When I, first of all, explained to Edith the meanings of the stones she had liked least, she laughed. Taking them in turn she explained to me that – referring to the tiger's eye – she had always been told, from her youngest days, what an independent person she was and, although this knowledge pleased her and she would hate to lose her own personal independence, as far as occupying her time was concerned, the last thing she wanted was isolation from people – she felt that she wanted to be *part* of something. With regard to the petrified wood, her late husband had been a

lawyer and there had been a period in her life when she had helped
in his office but, much as she had enjoyed it at the time, she felt
that what she wanted now was something totally different. She
had sufficient money and so was quite happy to work in some
voluntary capacity and she lived in a house that was full of books.
Although she was a great reader, she felt that her time should be
filled with people rather than with the printed word.

Having dealt with the stones Edith liked least – she would not
accept that she actually disliked them – I turned my attention to
the other group, the group that would give us some indication of
how she would be happiest to spend her time. There I found an
amethyst and a rose quartz. Now the presence of either of those
would have been sufficient to indicate a caring nature and a need
to be of service to others. The rose quartz itself is concerned with
healing, whether on an emotional or a physical level, and the
amethyst shows a spirituality and a genuine compassion. I felt that
this, coupled with Edith's stated need to be with people, was a
pointer to the fact that she would be happiest working in some
form of caring capacity.

I then went on to consider the remaining stones in that group.
They all seemed to be concerned with states of mind rather than
with physical conditions. There was the moss agate, showing
peace of mind, the turquoise, which means conentment and the
light green jasper, showing happiness. I told Edith that I thought
she would be extremely happy working with people and helping
them on some emotional level, bringing some sort of peace and
contentment into their minds and therefore to their lives.

The remaining stone was the aquamarine and this indicated to
me that Edith would be extremely good at helping such people
because she had a good, logical, feet-on-the-ground approach to
life in addition to the desire to be of assistance.

Edith agreed that she would really like to be able to help others.
Of course, she had done it all her life in her nursing career, but she
was no longer able to cope with the physical demands of that
particular life. She was terrified, she said, of being a do-gooder
who went around 'being nice' but achieving very little on a
practical level. But she said that she would think about what the
crystals and stones had indicated and would let me know what
transpired.

Edith wasted no time. So anxious was she to fulfil that part of her nature that was, as yet, unfulfilled that it was only a few days later when I heard from her. She telephoned to tell me that she would be working with a local voluntary organization, visiting old people and helping them to deal with their problems. These problems range from filling in forms to coping with bereavement – and everything in between. I could hear from her voice that Edith had found what she was looking for – and I am quite certain that she went on to be of great help to those who really needed her.

There are many, many instances of people who have been helped by crystals and stones to find a direction in life. Although I never tell them – nor, of course, will you – exactly what they should do, it is surprising how helpful they find it to be given pointers in particular directions or, sometimes, just some confirmation of their own inner thoughts – thoughts that might, at times, have seemed like little more than foolishness or wishful thinking. It is yet another example of a way in which your lovely crystals and stones will enable you to be of help to others.

Section IV

1. Conclusion

The examples set out in the previous section are all true case histories, the details of which have been taken from my files. Studying those examples closely should enable you to conduct a reading for yourself. But always remember, what I have set out there is the way in which *I* do *my* readings – you have your own personality, your own intuition, and it is quite possible that, over a period of time, you may adapt the method somewhat to suit yourself. There is no 'right' way or 'wrong' way – there is only the method which feels 'right' or 'wrong' to you. But the way that I have shown you is an excellent starting-point and one which will not let you down.

Obviously, before you can do anything at all, you have to learn the meaning attached to each and every crystal and stone that you possess. It is only when you know the basic relevance of each one that you can allow your intuition to guide you and to assist you in giving a more precise interpretation of what you see set out before you.

The intrinsic meaning of each stone remains constant. Naturally some variation in interpretation arises when one has regard to the surrounding crystals and stones selected. But there are no short cuts to familiarizing yourself with your own stones. You must curb your impatience and take your time. Friendships are not developed in a single day. Given time, your crystals and stones can become your greatest friends. When you meet an old friend in the street you are automatically certain not only of his name but of several facts about him. You do not have to wonder to yourself who he is or what type of life he leads. You *know*. In just the same way you should know all about your stones. If you pick up a piece of red jasper, for example, you should be instantly aware, without having to ask questions of yourself, that it represents love and deep emotion and that the more it is marked with green the more painful has been that emotion. When you are able to respond to each one of your crystals and stones in just the same way then – and only then – are you ready to commence reading from them.

There is no limit to the number of crystals and stones you can have in your own collection. What I have shown you in this book is really the minimum number you need to give any sort of intuitive reading. It is often a good idea, however, to have two, three or even several of a particular type. For one thing this will give the questioner a far greater choice and thus indicate to you far more clearly what is on his mind. For example, if your questioner selects nine stones of totally different type, even though there may be several of each in your collection, you will know that either he has several things on his mind at the time or that what he really requires is a reading which is general rather than specific. If, on the other hand, four or five of the stones are either of the same variety or of similar meaning, you will know that these relate to a particular subject which is occupying his mind at the time. If you only possess one of each type of stone to begin with, then the questioner's choice will of necessity be limited and he would not be able to indicate his preoccupation to you in the same way.

Another advantage of having more than one of some of the types of stone in one's collection is that it does help to give an idea of time. Take the amethystine agate, for example – the stone which indicates a move of home. I have several in my own collection and I have found that the larger the stone selected, the nearer in time that move of home will turn out to be.

Time, of course, is essentially a personal thing. I know readers who say that they can only give information concerning the next six months or so. Others will cover a lifetime if requested. This is something you will have to discover for yourself. I find that, using nine stones, my readings seem to cover a period of approximately two years. In fact I feel that the very nature of a reading from crystals and stones seems to limit one to this comparatively short period. This is one of the reasons why I do not give readings for young children. If a small child is living at home and attending school, there is very little change in that situation which is likely to occur within a two-year period.

Two years also seems to be an ideal period to cover. When I read from the stones that reading tends to give fairly detailed coverage of the first twelve months with a forecast of more general trends for the following year. Unless one's help is being sought in relation to a specific problem, it would seem pointless to give readings which cover just a few short weeks. On the other hand, since events in the far distant future will be greatly influenced by decisions made and action taken by the questioner himself in the interim period, to give a reading covering many years would seem to be an extremely difficult undertaking. It would often be so vague as to give little help to the questioner himself.

Crystals and semiprecious stones would seem to provide a reading on a more personal level than do many other methods of divination. Perhaps it is because the questioner actually selects the stones himself rather than just shuffling a pack of cards that his emotions, feelings, fears and hopes seem to be so clearly depicted in the reading. This is borne out by the fact that one would expect a person who likes – for example – pink and mauve crystals and stones always to select stones of that colour, however many times he has a reading. It just does not happen that way. I have several clients who come to me regularly – perhaps at intervals of three or four months – and they choose totally different types and colours of stone according to the mood they are in at the time and the problems which are then surrounding them.

Unless your questioner has some particular problem on his mind about which he requires help, I do not think it is a good idea for him to have readings more than three or four times a year at most. It will do no harm, but is unlikely to be much help either. Because we are working very much on an emotional level, there are unlikely to be vast alterations from one week to the next – except in the most exceptional of circumstances.

Crystals and semiprecious stones give you answers and information from the personal point of view of the questioner. They do not deal with national or worldwide events. Where they appear to refer to matters outside the personal life of the questioner, you will usually find that those matters do, in fact, have some considerable bearing upon his life. If a woman comes to you for a reading, it may well be that it is her husband who is about to have a change of employment in the near future but should that change of employment necessitate a move of home, for example, it will still show in your questioner's stones. The illnesses or anxieties of others will show up in a reading if those illnesses and anxieties touch upon the life of the questioner in some way. Perhaps he will have to spend some time caring for someone close to him. Perhaps there is some way in which he will become involved in the problems of another – or perhaps this is something he should take care to avoid.

Sometimes you will be asked, 'But what about my daughter?' or 'Can you tell me something about my wife?' The way to deal with this is to ask the questioner to sit quietly for a moment or two and focus the whole of his attention upon the person about whom he wishes to know more and, while still picturing that person, to choose a further five stones. In this way he will select the right stones to give you the information which you require.

How does it work? What makes someone choose the correct stones for a reading? We are working very much on a spiritual level and therefore help is coming from some force far greater than ourselves. If you accept that there is 'something' – whatever name you may choose to give to it, be it God, guide, spirit, fate or anything else – which leads a person who is shuffling a pack of tarot cards to shuffle them so that they appear in the right order, then that same 'something' will guide the one who has come to consult you to select the right stones for you to be able to tell him that which will be of the greatest assistance to him.

It is just for this reason – because we are working with something far greater than we ourselves – that we need to prepare not just our tools but also ourselves for the work we wish to do. Before you even begin to use your crystals and stones for healing or for divination you must prepare them well. This is not a time for impatience; each stage has to be methodically completed if you are to make the best use of nature's precious jewels. And the thorough cleansing and preparation of the gems will also give you time to get to know them better – and you must know them really well before you can help others. Look at your crystals and stones as you let the clear water run over them. Look at them again as they are allowed to dry naturally. Look and look until each one becomes a friend you would recognize in the same way that you recognize someone you have known for years.

It is not enough to cleanse and prepare your stones just once. Those which are to be used for readings will be handled quite frequently and so will need regular cleansing – just how often is up to you. But for one thing you would not wish them to lose their natural glow and lustre and, for another, if they are to be handled frequently you will want to re-purify them before they are used again.

Crystals and stones which are to be used for healing should be cleansed each time you use them if possible. After all, in this case you are actually seeking the help of their inherent force and energy and this must not be blocked by dust, dirt or grime. Nor would you want the vibrations left on the crystal by one whom you are treating to affect the next person who comes to you.

While you are preparing your stones and crystals, do not forget to prepare yourself for a reading too. It is essential that you learn to relax and to tune in to what your crystals and stones are telling you. If you know that you are to give a reading, take the time to be alone for a short while, close your eyes and – preferably holding that crystal which you have chosen to help you in your meditation – allow your mind to become free of all your own everyday problems so that you are best able to help the person who has come to consult you.

Remember, too, to make full use of your own psychic ability. You do have it – everyone has. You will have seen from the examples given in the previous section that the crystals and stones will provide you with the essentials of the reading – the bare bones. It is for you to supply the meat – the details which mean so much to the individual. You have to learn to be aware of, and to trust, your own intuitive skills. You will soon know whether you are using them correctly when you have feedback from those to whom you have given readings.

The crystals and stones will not let you down – and here is a story to prove it. Some time ago, when I was being interviewed for a magazine article about reading from stones, the young woman interviewing me asked whether I would mind some photographs being taken. As there was no one there apart from the two of us and the photographer, the interviewer sat with her back to the camera as if she were actually sitting at my table for a reading. The photographer – who was a complete disbeliever in any form of clairvoyance – wanted to make the picture look more authentic and so he picked up a handful of stones and dropped nine of them unceremoniously on the mat. While the photographs were actually being taken I talked to the journalist about the stones on the mat to make it appear that a reading was in fact taking place. When I had finished I looked up to see my interviewer laughing heartily. Apparently I had just described the young photographer and his immediate problems in great detail. So you see, even a disbeliever who took no care and no time in selecting the stones automatically chose the correct stones – the ones which would give him the background and answers to some of the problems then surrounding him.

In what way do you think of a psychic reading? Do you think that you are giving hard and fast answers to your questioner or do you feel that you are giving him guidance? I am convinced that the latter is the true way to approach what we do. I do not believe in absolute predestination and I do not think it is in our power – nor would it be desirable – to give those who come to us for help the idea that what we have to say to them is inevitable and unavoidable. What we are doing, you and I, is giving them an indication of the possibilities and trends which lie before them. We are not there to make decisions for others. At any stage in their lives – or indeed in your life or mine – they are free to change their direction, to make mistakes or to improve. I believe that throughout life one is put in a position where choices have to be made and, although by using the crystals and stones we get an insight into the emotions and personality of the questioner and therefore an indication of the type of choice he is likely to make, it is always his decision as to which path he will travel. I could say to someone during the course of a reading that I felt it likely that he would move home within the next year. The matter could proceed in that way, plans could be made, a van could be chugging away outside the front door and the person concerned could say, 'No, I have decided not to go.' That is his right.

It is never our job to make such decisions on behalf of another. I like to think that there is more to giving a reading than telling someone where the next boyfriend is likely to come from – I believe it is an indication of the good – and less good – trends which lie ahead and, hopefully, an indication of the type of decision the person will make. Because a reading from crystals and stones deals so much with the feelings and emotions of the individual rather than just with plain, cold facts, I also like to think that I send my questioners away with something to think about and also with hope for the future. By this I do not mean that I would tell anyone that which was untrue but that out of any situation one can either create that which is positive or that which is negative.

So now you have at your fingertips all the information you need to enable you to conduct psychic readings using crystals and semiprecious stones. Go forward now in honesty, faith and humility and you will have in your possession a very precious gift indeed – the means to be of help to your fellow man.

2. Information
Further reading on crystals and semiprecious stones:

Cosmic Crystals, by Ra Bonewitz (Turnstone Press); *Portals of Power*, by Win Kent and Jesse H. Thompson (published by the International Association of Colour Healers); *Precious Stones, Their Occult Power and Hidden Significance*, by W. B. Crow (Aquarian Press).

Suppliers of crystals and semiprecious stones:

Crystal World
PO Box 68
Gloucester GL4 9QB

Shambhala
10 South Molton Street
London W1

Crystal Light Centre

Craefte Supplies
33 Oldridge Road
London SW12

Crystal Research Foundation
37 Bromley Road
St Annes-on-Sea, Lancs.

Falcon Robinson
4 Rushbrook House
Union Grove
London SW8

'He answered, "I tell you if these were silent, the very stones would cry out."'
Luke 19:40

Index